Who Needs the Cuts?

Who Needs the Cuts?

Myths of the Economic Crisis

Barry Kushner and Saville Kushner

ɧ

Published by Hesperus Press Limited
28 Mortimer Street, London W1W 7RD
www.hesperuspress.com

First published Hesperus Press Limited, 2013
© Barry Kushner and Saville Kushner, 2013

Designed and typeset by Fraser Muggeridge studio
Printed and bound in Great Britain by CPI Group (UK) Ltd

ISBN: 978-1-84391-381-8

Contents

I
The Single Narrative
And Where It Came From

What is the use of repeating all that stuff, if you don't explain it as you go on? It's by far the most confusing thing I ever heard!
– *Alice in Wonderland*

Barry's Story

It was an unusually chilly July day when I arrived with a colleague in the small, proud but unmistakably impoverished town on the coastal fringe of north-west England. We had come for a meeting of the 'Children with Disabilities' planning group which we had been brought in to support.

A room was booked in a dilapidated ex-junior school that was accommodating the Children's Services offices. The meeting room, when we eventually found it, was in an ante-room off the old main hall that had all the feel of an equipment store.

Squeezed into this cramped space were local parents, representatives of voluntary sector organisations and council officers. Although the group was relatively new, its importance could not be overstated. For the first time in many years we had parents at the heart of the service planning process. They were coming together with both commissioners and providers to oversee the design, delivery and review of local services for their own children. This opportunity had been afforded by *Aiming High for Disabled Children*, a central government programme, based on sound evidence and articulating an ambitious vision for some of our most excluded and disadvantaged children. In practice, where I was working, this meant that the local network of parents was now actively leading on the design of a long-awaited respite care centre. But beyond the tangible, beyond the targets and measures, there was no mistaking the level of trust being slowly established between parents and professionals – a breaking-down of institutional barriers that had hampered partnership and progress for many years.

Sadly, the agenda for the meeting had changed at the last minute, so rather than giving an update on the capital project which I had been leading, I was now required to facilitate a discussion on how they had to abandon plans for the new centre.

This sudden change of plan was a direct result of the moratorium on spending that the incoming Chancellor, George Osborne, had introduced in his first 'emergency' budget. In May 2010 he had proudly announced that *'In the space of just a week, we have found and agreed to cut £6¼ billion of wasteful spending, across the public sector.'*[1] The respite care centre was a real example of Osborne's 'wasteful spending'. But why was he doing it? The Chancellor was clear and confident: *'We need to tackle the deficit so that our debt repayments don't spiral out of control.'*[2]

This is the kind of argument that we had been hearing since the inception of the new government, if not longer, and it amounts to a debt and deficit narrative that goes like this:

- Our national debt is higher than it's ever been
- Our deficit and debt interest payments are unmanageable
- Our debt crisis was caused by the overspending of the previous government
- We are on the brink of bankruptcy

The narrative was turned into simple mantras by Coalition government ministers, amplified by supporters in the media and embedded into the consciousness of the British people: 'The cost of repaying our debt is £120 million per day, we maxed out our credit card, our debt interest payments are higher than our spending on education, and the debt crisis was caused by Labour government overspending.'

The potency of this story, its ability to gain traction with ordinary people, is rooted in fear, anxiety and the almost effortless way in which the personal is woven into the national. The fear of financial meltdown – personal and national ruin. David Cameron had said it before, but repeated at the Davos get-together that Britain needed to cut its deficit or risk a full-blown fiscal crisis such as the one that has engulfed Greece. In June 2010, George Osborne told Andrew Marr: *'You can see in Greece an example of a country that didn't face up to its problems, and that is the fate that I want to avoid.'*[3] What is more, the Coalition was telling us that 'we are all in this together', the obvious connotation being that you are either 'with us or against us'.

In truth, all this comes close to what could be described as economic McCarthyism: tapping into fear and prejudice to drive a narrative aimed at establishing a level of acquiescence sufficient to force through a radical programme of action.

It is interesting to reflect that at the height of the witch hunt for communists in the United States in the 1950s, Senator McCarthy would hold up papers that he said contained lists of people whom he was investigating. In reality, we now know that there were often no lists of names; that his evidence was thin, but that the climate of fear he created was powerful enough to galvanise action and subdue challenge. It was a narrative that even the American president at the time found hard to resist, fearful of challenging in case the finger was pointed at him. In this way it disarmed people, stifled challenge and showed that you don't need cold hard evidence to build a compelling story. On the contrary, a powerful argument, statements that look like facts and the fear of consequences are quite sufficient.

In the same vein, the evidence tells us that our present debt narrative is just as much a construct of untested assertions, laced with fear. How bad would it be if there were no cuts? The government has made references to our economy ending up in the same position as that of Greece. After all 'we were on the brink of bankruptcy', George Osborne told us, and what's more the markets would abandon the UK: 'The largest bond investor in the world was saying that UK gilts were a no-go area, sitting on a bed of nitroglycerine.'[4] *Nitroglycerine.*

In the face of such scaremongering, no wonder we are made to feel awkward and risk being marginalised as heretics if we dare to even question the storyline. For example why, when our debt is lower than it has been in 200 of the last 250 years, when our borrowing is cheaper than it was during Thatcher's government, when unemployment and a decrease in taxation revenue has caused the deficit, are we told that the cuts are necessary and the only option? But more of that later.

Returning to the scene of the crime, the narrative started to build in the wake of the credit crunch in 2008, with bank bail-outs and an increase in unemployment. By the time the political parties were preparing for the autumn 2009 conference season, they were rehearsing arguments they were to take into the forth-coming election. Public sector spending cuts had become the main plank of Conservative Party policy and so it was for the Liberal Democrats, who even began to identify where the cuts would fall if they were in government. The Labour Party joined the cuts camp in full force slightly later, when Alistair Darling finally persuaded Gordon Brown and Ed Balls to change Labour Party policy in autumn 2009. Brown and Balls had been arguing that spending could be maintained if growth began to reduce the deficit – remember the media making hay with Gordon Brown's reluctance to utter 'the C-word'? Alistair Darling, James Purnell and others were arguing for cuts, and they won the day. By the time of the budget in March 2010, the Labour Party was committed to halving the deficit in four years. And Darling had confirmed in his interview with Nick Robinson about his March 2010 budget[5] that the cuts would be 'tougher and deeper' than those implemented by Thatcher's government in the 1980s.

This statement was a bombshell and the final confirmation that this debt story would see the country return to the divisive, unhappy period of the 1980s. Was that what we and our families and children had to look forward to? That period left its scars on us, as it has many baby boomers who lived through it. Austerity measures in the 1980s were met with marches, strikes, protests; Darling's offer to return to the 1980s was greeted with an intake of breath and a resigned nod of the head.

In December 2009, three months before Darling's statement, I had been at a reunion of the successful parent occupation of Croxteth Comprehensive in Liverpool. The school had been closed down in 1981, an early victim of Conservative Party cuts, and the parents' knee-jerk reaction had been to take over the school and open it up for their children. Three years later in 1984, after a campaign that brought together trade unions, educationalists, communities, musicians, actors and journalists, 'Crocky Comp' was re-opened. I was one of the campaigners and a teacher. The reunion was the first time the parents, some pupils and volunteer teachers and staff had come together to remember the successful campaign since then, and the heart of the event was an exhibition of photographs and a film retrospective of the events at the time.

In 1980 Croxteth was one of the poorest neighbourhoods in the country and the pictures brought it back: young people posing in the no-man's land of overgrown grass, dumped furniture and supermarket trolleys lying like tumbleweed in front of 1970s maisonettes, half of them empty and boarded up. The net result of cuts and limitations on social welfare in places like Croxteth was poor health, poor life chances for young people, few jobs and low life expectancy. Sean, who was a cute, cheeky, mischievous eleven-year-old when I taught him in 1983, was now forty, and had just stopped using drugs after twenty-eight years. He was taking me through the old school photograph, putting the names to the faces of the children who attended the school in 1983. At least seven were now dead.

Invoking the 1980s as the closest comparison to what was about to happen in the 2010s, this time with a political consensus, was shocking. Darling's statement was accepted by politicians and the media and absorbed into the inevitability of cuts. In fact Nick Robinson put the words in Alistair Darling's mouth:

> Robinson: The Treasury's own figures suggest deeper, tougher [cuts] than Thatcher's – do you accept that?
> Darling: They will be deeper and tougher.[6]

True, Robinson flushed out Darling's position, but where was his follow-up question about whether it was ethical or viable to return to a society that convulsed under the impact of austerity in the 1980s? 'Where we make the precise comparison, I think, is secondary to the fact that there is an acknowledgement that these reductions will be tough.' That was what Darling told us.

But how could that be the case? We all knew this began as a banking crisis that had its roots in the USA, with the mass sale of mortgages to people who couldn't afford them. These mortgages were consolidated into packages and sold on as investments to UK, American and other international banks, who in turn sold them on again, in large part to borrow money to finance re-mortgaging and 120 per cent mortgage deals in the UK. These are known as mortgage-backed securities. When homeowners in the USA began to default on their mortgages, the value these mortgage packages had as investments fell. When it came time for the banks to cash in these investments to return the money they had borrowed, they were worthless; the banks didn't have the cash to cover their own repayments and would have gone bust had governments in the UK, USA and other countries not stepped in and bailed them out.

The evidence was too strong and too well known by the British public for Mervyn King, the governor of the Bank of England, to walk away from. He knew cuts were coming; after all, he had taken the extraordinary step of planning government tax and spending policy with Cameron and Osborne prior to the election. He then took another extraordinary step of speaking to the Trades Union Congress (TUC) in 2010 to take the blame, and to soften us all up for public sector cuts: 'The billions spent bailing out the banks and the need for public spending cuts were the fault of the financial services sector.'[7] But if public spending was not the cause of the economic crisis, how can public sector cuts be the only solution? And why do we have to wait for a banker to tell us that?

Nevertheless, the narrative was getting through to the public. A *Daily Telegraph* poll[8] back in June 2009 had already recorded that seventy-five per cent of voters believed cuts were necessary. TUC polling throughout 2010 and 2011 consistently confirmed that most of the public felt the same, believing that there was no alternative. Indeed, the clamour of the debt narrative had drowned out dissenting voices and had now established a political consensus. A consensus that merely needed stating, often without recourse to analysis, let alone facts and (recent) history. The political parties were backed up by the Confederation of

British Industry (CBI), leading businessmen, the Centre for Economics and Business Research, the Governor of the Bank of England and by a number (though by no means all) of prominent economists. All were shouting for public sector spending cuts.

The narrative finally became government policy in May 2010, as the Conservative and Liberal Democrat Coalition picked up the reins of power. By October 2010 the government had issued the Comprehensive Spending Review, which translated the story into a reality of £80bn of public spending cuts. For you and for us, this means that certain operations and procedures are no longer available on the NHS, the poorest in our society are losing welfare benefits, police, nurses, social workers and teachers are cut back, and city councils like Liverpool's are losing £150m per year in a thirty per cent cut to their budgets. Sure Start centres and libraries are closing up and down the country, and the Institute of Fiscal Studies is forecasting that 600,000 more children will enter poverty. The list is endless, but it amounts to a fundamental structural change in the funding and delivery of public services, and a scale of shrinkage to our public sector never before seen. Will Hutton implored anyone who would listen to understand how extreme these cuts were:

No country has ever volunteered such austerity. It is as tough a package of retrenchment as the IMF imposed on Greece, a country on the brink of bankruptcy. It is twice as tough as the famously harsh measures Canada took between 1994 and 1997. It is three times tougher than Sweden's measures between 1993 and 1995. In British terms, it is immeasurably tougher than what we did after the IMF crisis in 1976 or after the ERM crisis in 1992... [9]

To explore this a little further, let's step back to where this chapter started, and my meeting with parents of children with disabilities, where I had to confirm that the capital programme had been closed and that the funds required to build the new respite care centre had been cut. The news was greeted with resignation. A parent representative was the first to respond, and given how proactive and uncompromising he and other parents had been in developing services for disabled children and the demands made on the council to provide facilities, I expected a tirade. I expected the council to be blamed for taking away the money or not spending it correctly, or calls to mount a campaign to have the programme reinstated. But no. He accepted the decision with resignation and said that in the face of 'overspending' there was little choice. The other parents and members of the meeting agreed. It was a devastating moment. I felt powerless to respond.

I had been working on this project for months and had witnessed the passion and commitment parents brought to the development of services for their disabled children. One parent broke down in tears at a meeting, out of the pain and frustration in trying to get across the need for the centre to give her and her family a respite break from their disabled daughter. The parent representatives on the planning group had gone into minute detail about the size of the rooms, the facilities and location of the centre. They had spent their own money travelling to meetings and volunteered their time to attend them. Over the previous ten years they had developed a confidence in their own views and opinions through having access to local policy and decision makers and their inclusion in decision-making – even about how money would be spent. They overcame their suspicion of local government and its officers, to work with them to develop facilities, after-school groups and support networks.

We caught a flavour of what this passion and moral purpose looks like on national TV when Jonathan Bartley,[10] the father of a disabled child, tackled David Cameron in the 2010 election campaign about his decision to close down special needs support in mainstream schools. Back at that planning meeting, I was witnessing at first hand how easily purpose and drive can be undermined and dissipated so much more quickly than it can be built up. In practice, the debt narrative was ploughing through people's ideals, ambitions and plans. No one else in the meeting disagreed with this parent, but all felt uncomfortable, powerless and lacking the necessary insight to frame a response.

It wasn't just people who attended the meeting who felt this way. The sense of powerlessness extended much further – arguably even to Alistair Darling. A lot of people felt helpless to challenge the cuts because the debt narrative was so overwhelming. As my brother and I became active in promoting resistance to cuts we saw people fall into three broad categories of response: those who agreed with the debt analysis of the necessity for cuts; those who were resigned and felt that there was no alternative; and those who disagreed with the cuts out of the sense that the rationale was political and not economically driven, but couldn't marshal a coherent argument.

The sovereign debt and spending-cuts narrative was cemented. The only difference between the political parties now boiled down to how many billion pounds were to be cut and over how many years. It was a matter of degree, not substance. The media picked this up and ran with it.

Students, in the first challenge to government cuts, marched against the increase in university tuition fees. What reporters wanted to know was where the cuts would fall if more money were put into university education to bring down the level of fees. BBC's *Question Time* became a national, weekly platform for the debt narrative. Almost every discussion on almost any topic whether it be defence, schools, international development or sport followed a similar pattern. Government ministers and supporters argued that with the 'mess' they were left by the previous government there was no alternative to the political decisions the government was taking. Cuts were in the national interest. More often than not the Labour Party representatives remained quiet, uncomfortable and unable to challenge.

There was no better evidence of the predominance of the new consensus than the media build up to the Comprehensive Spending Review in October 2010. National and regional BBC radio stations, Sky and ITV national news, local and national press were asking readers, viewers and listeners to make suggestions as to where the cuts should fall. This didn't happen in the 1980s when there were alternative and competing arguments and analyses. So why is there no challenge to this now? In the 1980s the decisions to make public sector spending cuts were clearly political. In 2010, the need for cuts was a given and our leading journalists were seduced by the argument. John Humphrys prefixed his interview with Nick Clegg in the week before the CSR with the words 'We know you need to make cuts, but...' Andrew Marr followed this up in his keynote inquisition of George Osborne: 'You clearly need to make the savings, the cuts and raise taxes...' He even allowed Osborne's historic, unprecedented assertion that the country was on the brink of bankruptcy to go unchallenged.

Even Andrew Tyrie, the Conservative chair of the Treasury Select Committee, did better than Marr. He told George Osborne that talk of bankruptcy was *'over-egging it'*.[11] But a distinctive feature of the coverage of the debt narrative has been the mainstream media's largely unquestioning acceptance of government statistics and political assertions about the economy.

Stephanie Flanders, economics editor at the BBC, in her report of 9 September 2011, put the reason for poor growth figures down to the good weather, the tsunami in Japan and the day off for the Royal Wedding. Why did she not mention that the retail sales and manufacturing slump, combined with redundancies as a result of spending cuts, were starting to have an impact, and consumer confidence was at an all-time low? 'We were providing the explanation provided by the ONS, the independent statistical body,' Stephanie wrote.[12] Yet her role in the BBC is analysis, not news reporting. Her unquestioned reproduction of a government/ONS press release is closer to her previous role as speechwriter and advisor to Larry Summers than that of the BBC's chief analyst. (She had also worked with the US Treasury Secretary, as he presided over the deregulation of the banking system that unleashed the whirlwind of mortgage-backed securities, credit default swaps, sub-prime mortgages and over-leveraged banks that sit behind the whole debt issue.) 'If this was not emphasised yesterday, that was simply because there were other things to focus on in a 2.5 minute package, and the broad political and economic arguments about austerity are now so well understood by our viewers.'[13] I was referred to her blog.

What was worse, any challenge to the debt narrative was now being questioned in moral terms. Martha Kearney accused Hilary Benn of being a 'deficit denier' and the Conservatives had singled out Ed Balls as the number one 'deficit denier'. This is emotive, powerful language redolent of attacks on Holocaust 'deniers' and used regularly to dismiss argument and debate about climate change. There is no way of understanding 'deficit denier' other than its suggestion that challenging the debt narrative is immoral. In fact it was denying the British public a debate. Without as much information as possible being placed in the public domain, how can we make judgements, ask intelligent questions, be sceptical, come up with other solutions? Never mind the fiscal deficit – the debt narrative has created a democratic deficit.

In our desperation, my brother and I started to write to the BBC and to *The Guardian* to complain about the coverage of debt and the lack of challenge to the debt narrative. We made the point in a series of emails and interventions on radio phone-ins that although the coverage reflected the political consensus it did not reflect the broader economic analysis represented by numerous economists and people on both sides of the political spectrum. We crystallised our scepticism into a Powerpoint presentation and gave talks wherever we could. We begged the question, doesn't the BBC have a duty to do this?

'The Editorial Guidelines state that we strive to reflect a wide range of opinion and explore a range and conflict of views so that no significant strand of thought is knowingly unreflected or under-represented,' a senior executive at BBC News told us. She almost sounded as though she may have been agreeing with us, until she went on to write: 'However, reflecting a broad range of views is not the same as giving equal weight to all shades of opinion and nor are we required to give totally comprehensive coverage.'

That even appears to be the case when journalists know that there is more to add to an analysis. Evan Davis had given Len McCluskey, the Unite union general secretary, a grilling on the radio, unlike anything to which Danny Alexander, George Osborne or other government ministers had been subjected. We wrote to Evan Davis to ask him why he prevented McCluskey from elaborating on his argument and why he didn't challenge ministers in the same way. For example, we asked, why are ministers not asked to explain the significance of the low level of national debt and borrowing on their cuts planning? He replied:

I personally think there are arguments to be made for not dealing with the deficit at the moment. Indeed there are arguments for monetising it too. But these need to be set out by those who want to assert them not by me.[14]

So Evan knows the answers, but won't tell us what they are? Aren't journalists supposed to use their knowledge and experience to ask more intelligent, searching questions?

Given the scale of the cuts and the fundamental shift in the delivery of public services, there has been very little sustained resistance. The students kicked it off in the autumn and winter of 2010 with a large demonstration in London against an increase in university tuition fees that included attacking the Conservative Party HQ in Millbank. Many of us, desperate to resist the cuts agenda, pinned our hopes on them. 'Students did it in France in 1968, China and the USA in the 1960s,' some thought. But their resistance dissipated as the New Year began, the police relentlessly hunted down prominent demonstrators, and the courts imposed explicitly deterrent penalties. The trade unions were starting to push an alternative to cuts agenda, led by the Public and Commercial Services Union, but they were nervous to go straight for strikes and be picked off as an isolated resistance to the government. Anyway, they were not sure the members were ready to go on strike. The TUC polling and the growing power of the narrative told them that. The unions didn't want to go it alone and Brendan Barber announced that 'the TUC is keen to build the widest possible coalition against the cuts, involving unions, charities, community groups and faith organisations'.[15] The unions funded the False Economy website, which collected information that challenged the debt narrative and was trying to build an alliance with the other sectors.

The Culture Secretary, Jeremy Hunt, visited Liverpool to open an exhibition in the Walker Museum. The full scale of the cuts had already been revealed by George Osborne, and this was almost the first opportunity to show a minister of state how we felt about it. What's more the art gallery is less than a Usain Bolt sprint from the Unite north-west regional office. My wife and I hadn't joined a demonstration since the 1980s, when tens of thousands turned out whenever there was a march or a protest. In 1983, at the height of the Liverpool City Council confrontation with the Conservative government over deep cuts to the city budget, Tony Benn, Arthur Scargill and Derek Hatton led marches that stopped the city and filled the streets with noisy, angry chanting.

We walked across the St George's Hall Plateau and across the cobblestones to the foot of the gallery steps, where the police had put tape up to prevent anyone entering the Walker Gallery. There were about thirty other people there, and no one was sure if the Culture Secretary had already gone into the building or if they would see him. Where was everyone else?

In May 2011 we joined the Alternative march along the embankment to Hyde Park in London. It was the alliance that Brendan Barber, the General Secretary of the TUC, had spoken of, and more than 500,000 people were there. There was singing, salsa bands playing, chatting. It was a polite demonstration. UK Uncut organised flashmobs of tens of people targeting shops and banks that do not pay their fair share of tax, and the Occupy movement was spreading from London across the UK's major cities. But this was unconnected activity, disparate, almost like a suite of protest choices from which people could choose the cause that best suited them. Though welcome and at times challenging, it did not feel as though they were building a momentum towards a counter-narrative.

So that's the state of affairs: inadequate challenge to the debt narrative by journalists and no alternative represented by a mainstream political party – parents accepting services for their disabled children will get worse, Croxteth facing a return to the poverty of the 1980s and the majority of the public believing that cuts are inevitable. There isn't even the political satire of Spitting Image to tease out the inconsistencies and absurdities in government policy.

With little political leadership, how can an alternative analysis be developed? We couldn't stand by and watch this happen and in June 2010, together with my brother I started to look into this more deeply. We were following up clues that we had picked up in the letters pages of national newspapers. Sixty economists told us that 'the current deficit reflects the deepest and longest global recession since the war, with extraordinary public sector fiscal and financial support needed to prevent the UK economy falling off a cliff'. Not only that, they also told us that in their opinion the debt narrative is a scare tactic: 'They seek to frighten us with the present level of the deficit but mention neither the automatic reduction that will be achieved as and when growth is resumed nor the effects of growth on investor confidence.'[16]

Twenty other economic historians made a plea to change the substance of the debate by placing the debt crisis in the context of previous economic crises, namely that our national debt has been higher for most of the last 250 years, and that the global deregulation of banks and the assumption that governments will bail them out has created ever greater economic crises. Instead of cuts, they argued, the government should 'turn their attention to promoting the economic growth that can speed up the repayment of public debt'.[17]

These were just two letters to national newspapers, but when we were looking for evidence to challenge the debt narrative, there was no mainstream source of information to build on. The case put by eighty economists did not enter the political discourse, and I cannot remember hearing a politician make any reference to their claims. In the event, the May 2010 General Election passed without any mention of these pleas for economic balance and debate. No wonder the people I worked and socialised with had no information to work on to raise questions about the cuts – not even economists in the business school of my brother's university.

The UK's own economics Nobel Prize winner in 2010 told us that 'the Chancellor has exaggerated the sovereign risks that are threatening the country'.[18] That was virtually a repeat of Andrew Tyrie's[19] 'over-egging' statement, but it was not repeated elsewhere. This alternative analysis was restricted to the small print of reporting on the economic crisis – on blogs, in short references in articles and in news reports, but it was not granted the balance of analysis that its challenging views represented. We have heard few journalists refer to this alternative analysis in challenging government or Labour Party statements on cuts – we will look at that in the final chapter.

In June 2010 Saville, my brother, had given a public lecture in Bristol on the impact of cuts on our democracy. He looked for data on the scale of the economic 'crisis'. He could find none at all that spoke convincingly of any crisis and reported that to the amazement of his audience. Intrigued, fired with a sense that we could do something other than swallow what was happening and march ineffectually, we both trawled the internet through government official statistics, the Treasury website, the CIA World Factbook, economics articles, interviews on YouTube, speeches and Select Committee meetings and online economics lectures. We spoke to economists and journalists, and we began to put facts and figures together and build up a picture of deficit, taxation, banks, GDP and debt that told a different story to the narrative, one that was strongly suggestive of an alternative to the assertion that the UK was in economic 'crisis'. In fact, the information we found suggested that our economy was in a fit enough state to cope with the debt and deficit problems we were experiencing as a result of the 2008 recession. Our debt is relatively low, our deficit can be financed by cheap borrowing, and growth can bring the deficit down.

We put all this into a PowerPoint slideshow, sending it through our contact database, encouraging recipients to do the same, and we started giving public talks, one of which you can see on YouTube and another on Bristol Indymedia.[20] We disseminated many thousands of copies of the presentation in the form of a card-set – UNISON used it in their representative training – and we even spoke to Ed Balls and his shadow treasury team.

One of the first things we found was that there are key phrases, commonly used, that none of us really understand and are rarely explained. What is GDP? What is a deficit? Can it be structural and what does that mean anyway? What is quantitative easing? What is UK debt? What are the implications of inflation and what is it? By the 1990s, there turned out to be more than one definition of it – Retail Price Index or Consumer Price Index. What are they? How do they differ? And what difference does it make if they do?

Not many of us feel comfortable talking about economics, mainly because it it is made to sound so complicated and scientific. Its vocabulary alone is intimidating – and not just to the public. Senior Labour politicians told us that even Labour MPs are afraid of talking about economics and tend to avoid the subject. They even avoid attending briefings, so no wonder *Question Time* is always a debt narrative whitewash.

But there is an alternative narrative and it is accessible and understandable, even in economic terms. There is an explanation of the economic events of the past five years that does not describe a UK in debt crisis. It offers choice, differences of opinion, uncertainty, and hope. It takes us on a different voyage beyond economics into politics and visions of society, our expectations and ambitions, and into an understanding of why the American Nobel prize-winning economist Paul Krugman wrote 'Jobs now, deficits later was and is the right strategy. Unfortunately, it's a strategy that has been abandoned in the face of phantom risks and delusional hopes.'[21]

II
Debt, Love and History

The problems we face are big and urgent – rebuilding our broken economy – because unless we do, our children will be saddled with debt for decades to come.
– David Cameron

It is 4 November 2010, and George Osborne is giving evidence to the Treasury Select Committee in the Wilson Room at Portcullis House. The Chancellor is there to account for the decisions he made in the Comprehensive Spending Review a couple of weeks before. And what is that by the way? 'A Treasury-led process to allocate resources across all government departments, according to the government's priorities,'[22] so the Treasury informs us. It sets the spending and tax priorities over a number of years. The Select Committee's job is to scrutinise it.

The Chancellor had told us what his economic and public priorities were in his speech to the House of Commons on 21 October: 490,000 public sector jobs to be lost, the consequence of £80bn of cuts to the public sector in four years. Why? Because, as he told Andrew Marr three weeks before, 'we are on the brink of bankruptcy'. We watched in disbelief at the scale of what Osborne was proposing, a bit like watching someone give you an injection. You don't want it, you know it's going to happen, but there is no stopping it. Most of the country probably thought that, except that when he sat down after his speech the benches behind him cheered and waved their order papers. It seemed too much even for Alan Johnson, the Labour Party shadow chancellor, and he couldn't help but break ranks with the cuts narrative for a second when he observed that 'for some members opposite, this is their ideological objective... For many of them this is what they came into politics for.' Actually, his divergence from the cuts narrative didn't last long. The next day on the *Today* programme on Radio 4 Alan Johnson was being interviewed about the comment he had made in the commons that day before, and he was back-tracking. He didn't want to create the ideological divide, and the narrative washed over us again.

Back in Portcullis House, and the Chancellor has confidently brushed off criticisms of his budget, answering with facts, suppositions and statements to back up his case. Debt is unsustainable, so is the deficit; our AAA credit rating is under threat, he is telling us. He is talking fluently, bristling with figures, until it comes to the Labour member of the committee, John Mann's turn to ask a question:

'The national debt, that we have, is the highest in our history?'

You can see that Osborne doesn't want to answer that question directly: 'It is in cash terms,' he replies.

The Chancellor lifts his head to the side, looks away from the committee, takes a breath and hesitantly answers. He starts to stare into the distance, as if he is concentrating, trying to come up with an answer. After all, his previous Comprehensive Spending Review and his previous answers to the Treasury Select Committee were peppered with precise information and data on all aspects of the economy, at the heart of which is the public debt.

John Mann persists; he has spotted an evasive answer. 'Is this the highest in your lifetime?'

'It is [pause] err.' He starts and then stops, nods his head very slightly four times as if he is agreeing something with himself. He raises his eyebrows as he lifts his head up and looks at John Mann again. 'No doubt you are about to tell me.'

But it couldn't be that our most senior economic minister does not know the answer. The questioning continues.

'Italy, France, Germany, Japan, the United States and the United Kingdom. Of those six, which has the lowest national debt today?'

'Well. [pause] What I would point out... Well as I say Mr Mann. [pause] The answer is the United Kingdom.'

Hang on. This is starting to get confusing. It seems that there is more to the debt issue than we were first told. We had not heard any comparison of our debt with other countries in the political arena before, or the suggestion that our debt has been higher in our history.

But let's get back to basics. A lot of the economic analysis, particularly debt, revolves around using common economic terms. Speaking to friends, watching the television, listening to the radio, commentators and politicians, everyone talks about GDP, debt, deficit. But what are these things? What do they mean? In fact how can we get involved in any debate about our economy without understanding what these terms actually mean?

GDP looks like a good place to start and Declan Curry, the former BBC business editor agrees: 'Gross Domestic Product is arguably the most important of all economic statistics as it attempts to capture the state of the economy in one number.'[23] GDP stands for Gross Domestic Product, basically the value in pounds of everything that we earn as a country in one year. Investopedia calls it 'the monetary value of all the finished goods and services produced within a country's borders in a specific time period, though GDP is usually calculated on an annual basis'. The Economics About Dictionary tells us it is 'the market value of all the goods and services produced by labour and property located in the region, usually a country'.[24] The Financial Dictionary uses fewer words, but more or less describes the same thing: 'A measure of the value of the total production in a country, usually in a given year.' [25]

When you look at how GDP is calculated, these definitions start to make more sense. It is made up of four things:

1. Consumer spending: everything that consumers spend on goods and services in the course of one year
2. Business investment: everything that businesses invest in buildings and machinery in the course of one year
3. Government spending: the value of the goods and services the government buys
4. The value of everything we export minus the value of everything we import

When you add all the figures up from each category above, you end up with the country's GDP. But who adds all this up and from where does the government get these figures? Actually, GDP is estimated every quarter by a survey conducted by the Office for National Statistics. Information on sales is collected from a questionnaire survey of 6,000 companies in manufacturing, 25,000 service sector firms, 5,000 retailers and 10,000 companies in the construction sector. That is 46,000 businesses. If you add up all businesses registered to pay VAT, all sole traders, partnerships, charities, a survey of 46,000 companies represents less than one per cent of the total number of businesses trading in the UK. And that doesn't include businesses in the grey sector. But nevertheless, on the basis of what is basically a survey, GDP is presented not as an estimate, but as a *gold-plated fact*.

When commentators, economists and politicians talk about a percentage of economic growth, they mean the amount of extra GDP there has been in the course of the year or in a quarter. The extra amount of GDP is then turned into a percentage of the total figure of GDP and that is our figure for growth. So if GDP was £100bn and there were an increase of £3bn that would be described as three per cent growth.

GDP growth is calculated – or rather estimated – every quarter (three months), and is reported on the news when it is announced by the Treasury. In the past twenty years growth has tended to vary from zero to two per cent per quarter. But as with any statistics, what is the margin of error there? Electoral party polling is also a survey, but this has a margin of error of three per cent higher or lower than the polling figures we are given. That is a six per cent range. That begs the question of what the margin of error is for calculating GDP. Does anyone tell us that? It turns out that this figure, which is the baseline economic figure for our economy, is, indeed, an *estimate*.

Accurate or not, this is all we have to work with, and not just here but across the world. So the latest estimated figure in the UK for our annual GDP, when you add it all up, and as this book goes to print is £1,552bn. That is the seventh highest GDP in the world; only the USA, Germany, China, Japan, India and Russia have a GDP greater than ours. That makes us a rich and high-turnover country.

Back to George Osborne. He is now sitting in Andrew Marr's studio on a Sunday in October 2010, the week before he was to announce the results of his Comprehensive Spending Review and tell the nation 'we were on the brink of bankruptcy' and [26] the Prime Minister told us his priority was 'Rebuilding our broken economy – because unless we do, our children will be saddled with debt for decades to come.' [27] Alistair Darling had already told us in December 2009 that the level of debt was so high that it would mean cuts greater than Margaret Thatcher's: 'We have to be realistic – the spending environment will be tough over the next few years.'[28]

It was going to take a generation for us to get over this, we were told. We have children, and this was making us think that they would have a grim future. All the things that we had enjoyed, like free healthcare, a job, welfare benefits, our own house, a car and enough money to pay for petrol, they would struggle to obtain. It made us feel like some or all of these things would be beyond them. The debt storytellers were painting a picture of our children's future that was Dickensian and grim. Is it really our children and your children that are going to have to pay for this?

The UK Debt Bombshell website, a blog, which records the level of debt on a daily basis, puts a figure on it.[29] On 11 October 2012 it told us that 'we owe £16,550 for every man, woman and child... That's more than £36,257 for every person in employment.' With the average wage at about £25,000, that means the debt per head is about sixty-six per cent of the average wage. And it doesn't stop there – UK Debt Bombshell dropped another one: 'Every household will pay £1,935 this year, just to cover the interest.' We didn't know that we were paying off the debt interest *ourselves*.

Of course we are not individually liable for the repayment of government debt. The government is. Debt is not broken down into small amounts for individuals or households to pay. It is held by the government on our behalf and paid through the use of our taxes, and that is so that each of us is not *personally* liable for the national debt. In the same way that we do not individually pay for a hospital or a school, because that too is funded through public expenditure. We pay our taxes into the public purse or the Treasury, and these financial transactions are paid for from it. It is misleading to suggest that we will receive a bill at the end of the year to cover our individual part of the national debt.

Besides, when Barry was born in 1961 the national debt was about £28bn. Continuing with the same logic as applied by the Debt Bombshell website and David Cameron, as the population in 1961 was 53 million, that meant that every man, woman and child owed £528. The average salary then was £799 per year, so the debt per head was about sixty-six per cent of the average wage. That is about the same as it is today, but we were then in a period when Prime Minister Macmillan told us we had never had it so good. So it looks like our parents left us debt to pay, just as we are leaving our children debt to pay and that our debt per head is about the same now as it was in 1961. *Now that is a bombshell.*

But what is debt anyway? 'Government debt is the stock of outstanding IOUs issued by the government at any time in the past and not yet repaid. Governments issue debt whenever they borrow from the public; the magnitude of the outstanding debt equals the cumulative amount of net borrowing that the government has done.'[30] In other words our national debt is the equivalent to the total amount that the government currently owes or borrows. This is called Public Sector Net Debt.

This has become slightly more complicated, as the government has an additional calculation of public sector debt, which includes the borrowing the government has made to pay for financial interventions. Since the banking crisis this has risen considerably, so this calculation can add an additional £300–400bn to our debt figure.

The Treasury, however, prefers to use the measurement of debt that excludes ('ex') financial support to banks, because 'when calculating the ex measures, the key is to identify whether transactions and balance sheet positions are temporary effects of the financial crisis that will be eventually reversed, or whether they are permanent'.[31] The Treasury considers these payments to the banks short-term measures that will be repaid when the banks are resold, or as banks repay the loans through fees and repayments to the government. As such, it believes that these investments, insurance schemes and bail-outs will not add to the national debt in the long term, and excludes them from the calculation of Public Sector Net Debt.

Other commentators also use a wider figure for debt that includes the public cost of borrowing that was used to build schools, hospitals and other government buildings through private finance initiatives. This raises public debt to more than £2,200bn. But again this falls under the Treasury's test of whether they add to the debt in the long term, and as these loans are financed by school and hospital budgets, expensive and ill-judged as they may have been, they are not financed by public borrowing, so this falls into the 'excluding financial interventions' category.

In the political arena, ministers and opposition spokespeople use figures for debt that vary according to the measures used to calculate it. The government, the last Labour and the current Coalition one, uses the debt figure excluding financial interventions, whereas in opposition the Conservatives tended to use the higher figure that included financial interventions. But the Treasury is quite clear that 'temporary effects on PSNB [Public Sector Net Borrowing] or PSND [Public Sector Net Debt] need to be removed when moving to the ex measures; permanent effects that are not captured as a result of removing the temporary effects need to be specifically included'. That excludes financial interventions to bail out the banks, PFI and other financial measures, which means that it is the Treasury that uses that excluded figure, so it is the one we will use. It is also a figure that is comparable to the calculation of debt throughout our history and the way our trading partners calculate debt.

But What is Debt and Who Owns It?

The vast majority of national debt is borrowing through the issue of government bonds. In simple terms, the government is lent money for a fixed period of time and in exchange lenders are offered a fixed guaranteed annual interest payment and the repayment in full of the amount lent when the bond matures at the end of the fixed term. The bonds that the government issues are called 'gilts' and there is a constant flux of gilts – some mature and need repaying and, at the same time, new ones are issued. We will use the word bonds from now on. For example a bond worth £100,000 that was issued ten years ago will mature today, which means the government will have to pay back to the lender £100,000. It may then need to issue another bond of the same value to replace it, and another bond is issued to the value of £100,000 for another ten years. So as one bond matures, another one is issued.

All of this is managed through the Debt Management Office (DMO), which is a department of the Treasury. The amount of money that the government will borrow in any one year is set in the annual budget, as the Chancellor of the Exchequer calculates what the difference will be between public spending and income (mainly from taxation). If there is a gap between the two, it will be financed by borrowing, and borrowing, as described above, is financed by bonds, and the DMO will work out a schedule of what bonds need to be issued through the year.

The amount of interest that government needs to pay a lender every year, and the length of time that the government will keep the money before the bond matures, depends on how credit-worthy lenders consider the government to be. But as the UK has always made every single payment on the bonds it has ever issued since 1692, our bonds are considered to be a very good bet.

But what this means is that debt is dynamic and is constantly being recycled as bonds are maturing and new ones are being issued throughout the year by the DMO. UK Debt Bombshell, our politicians, most economists and media commentators talk about national debt as if it is a fixed lump sum. It is not. In effect, a bond paid today is being replaced by a bond that doesn't have to be repaid for ten or fifteen years. That is future debt.

At the time of writing, our debt is around £1,006bn. But to whom do we owe money? Who buys UK government bonds? Almost forty per cent of government bonds have been bought by UK insurance companies, pension funds and other financial institutions. The government also owes around £375bn to the Bank of England. As the Bank of England is a branch of the government, of the £1,006bn debt that we have, £375bn of it, or almost one-third, is owed to ourselves. As a country we owe around thirty-one per cent of our debt to other financial institutions and banks overseas, which means that most of our debt, almost seventy per cent, is UK-owned.

This is a different to situation from that in, say, Greece, which owes over fifty-six per cent of its debt to foreign institutions – one reason, by the way, that the UK is nothing like Greece. Portugal, Ireland and Spain, incidentally all have more than seventy per cent of their debt owned by foreign banks and private financial institutions.

Debt As a Percentage of GDP

We have been given the impression that it will take a generation to put us on our feet again, such is the level of public debt that we face. And the figures are scary. But how do we really make a judgement as to whether £1,006bn is too high or low, manageable or unmanageable, significant or insignificant? We are conscious that the level of debt is not put into any wider economic or historical context. And anyway, how can we make a judgement about this?

Well the starting point is to look at debt as a percentage of GDP. Why? The best way of explaining this is to take an example of, say, bread. A loaf of bread in 1970 cost 9p,[32] but costs about £1.25 today. How do we know which is more expensive? The simplest way is to compare both prices as a percentage of the average wage in both years. In 1970 the average wage was £32 per week, so a loaf was 0.28 per cent of that wage, whereas the average wage today is about £470[33], making a loaf 0.26 per cent of average salary. That makes a loaf of bread slightly cheaper today than it was in 1970.

It is the same with debt. The simplest way of making a comparison of how high debt is between one year and another, is to compare it as a percentage of GDP. The Treasury uses this itself: 'Debt measures are usually presented as a percentage of GDP since comparisons over time need to allow for effects such as inflation.'[34] If GDP is £1,552 bn, that makes our debt sixty-five per cent of the value of all we earn in a country in one year. Now we know that we can make comparisons with Europe, our own history of debt, and against our main trading partners.

For most of the period of the last government, national debt was around forty-two per cent of GDP, and rose as a result of government borrowing, the credit crunch and the banking crisis to a peak of fifty-seven per cent in November 2010. It has actually only risen to sixty-five per cent in the first few months of 2012. The fact that our debt hovers around sixty per cent is significant, because this is the level that the EU set as a maximum for debt when Margaret Thatcher signed the Maastricht Treaty on 7 February 1992. That means that, even though UK debt has risen, for most of this period of economic crisis it has been below the EU benchmark, one of the few countries in the EU where that is the case. In fact. if you deduct the £375bn that the Bank of England has lent, then debt would be around forty per cent of GDP.

UK National Debt As Percent Of GDP
UK Public Spending from FY 1900 to FY 2010

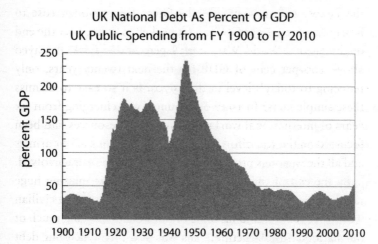

ukpublicspending.co.uk

Debt in the UK has been higher than it is now in 200 out of the last 250 years. British economic historians tried to bring this to our attention in their letter to *The Guardian* in March 2010 prior to the last election. It was a *crie de coeur* from them to make us look at the history of debt and put current debt into perspective:

> History shows, first, that British public debt is not high by the standards of the last 200 years. It is rather low in comparison to the second half of the 18th century, the first three-quarters of the 19th century, and most of the interwar and post-second world war era in the 20th century. It is also low in the context of the developed world.[35]

Our politicians across the spectrum and the media didn't pick this up, and by the end of 2012 most were still of the opinion that debt is unsustainably high. What were they missing?

When we look at the history of debt over the last 100 years we can see that our debt now is as low as it has been since before the 1920s. As we went into the Great Depression it rose to nearly 170 per cent of GDP, and it peaked in 1947, after the end of the Second World War, at 238 per cent of GDP. It stayed above 100 per cent of GDP for the next twenty years, only reducing to today's level in the 1970s. Is it so easy to dismiss these simple facts? In 1947 our country was emerging from six years of international warfare. Most of our resources had been focussed on the war effort, paying for the millions in our armies and all the weapons production and logistics that were involved.

By the end of the war we were not only demobilising huge numbers of servicemen and reintegrating them into the civilian workforce, but rebuilding some of our major cities and much of our national infrastructure. This was at a time when our debt was 238 per cent of the value of our GDP and we still built the welfare state, national pensions, mass higher education, free, universal secondary education, a motorway network and council housing.

Public Sector Net Debt is not something that was created in the last five to ten years or by the last Labour government. National debt started in 1692 and has risen almost every year since then.

Debt didn't go down well at that time either, by the way. David Hume, one of our first ever economists, was incensed that 'our modern expedient, which has become very general, is to mortgage the public revenues, and to trust that posterity will pay off the incumbrances contracted by their ancestors'.[36] Sound familiar? This is the 'we are passing debt onto our children' argument that David Cameron has made. But Hume was writing in 1742.

How did this debt come about? William III was king and was attempting to rebuild the country and the Royal Navy after the Glorious Revolution of 1688 and the French victory at Beachy

Head in 1690. The king feared a French invasion, but didn't have the money to build a new navy himself and needed to find £1,200,000. So he pulled together a group of wealthy merchants and formed a national bank. The bank would lend the king the money he needed, in exchange for the bank holding and administering government finances. This became incorporated as the Bank of England and its first lending is the first recorded time that the government borrowed money – the first ever public debt. In fact, this is the first recorded occasion that any government in the world went into debt to finance its activities.

Debt rose from there to finance the Marlborough's wars, wars against the French, against the North American colonial rebels, and peaking in 1815 at the end of the Napoleonic Wars at over 200 percent of GDP.[37]

David Hume was so appalled at this borrowing and the increasing debt that he went on to predict this situation would erode the very fabric of the country: 'Either the nation must destroy public credit, or public credit will destroy the nation.'[38] He was convinced that the pressure of paying the debt would fall on individuals, who would be less likely to work and trade as a result. People would even start fighting each other. Weighing up the likely impact of public debt, he felt the country would disintegrate, claiming that 'it is more probable, that the breach of national faith will be the necessary effect of wars, defeats, misfortunes, and public calamities'.[39] If Andrew Marr had been there to interview him at the time, David Hume would surely have said that the country in 1742 was on the brink of bankruptcy.

Thomas Babington Macaulay, a nineteenth-century English historian, had the benefit of hindsight, as he too looked at the impact that debt could have had on the country, but with the advantage of writing nearly 100 years later. He noted in *The*

History of England in 1848 that the country's debt that Hume had written about in 1692 was £1m. When Hume wrote 'Of Public Credit' in 1752, it had increased to £76.9m, and when Macaulay wrote the *The History of England*, debt was a mighty £780m. Macaulay was living proof that the country had survived this borrowing.

In fact the UK had survived war, internal strife, social breakdown and bankruptcy, much as we did in 1947 when, remember, debt was 238 per cent of GDP. Macaulay caustically dismissed the predictions and the doom-laden warnings of contemporary politicians in light of industrial and social advances, pointing out that 'while the shallow politicians were repeating that the energies of the people were being borne down by the weight of the public burdens the first journey was performed by steam trains'. So this is not the first time we have witnessed a moral panic over debt. It has ever been thus, as debt has increased year by year, decade by decade, century by century, so have the prophets (and the profits) of doom.

Our Debt is Lower than that of our Trading Partners

Not only is UK public debt more or less within EU limits: it is also lower than the debt of our major trading partners. Compared to our current debt-to-GDP ratio of sixty-five per cent, Germany's is seventy-nine per cent, France's is eighty-five per cent, the USA's is 101 per cent and Japan's is a whopping 228 per cent.

What is noticeable is that the relationship between debt and the economic performance of each country appears to be quite random. For example, Brazil (fifty-nine per cent) and India (fifty-seven per cent) have similar debt-to-GDP ratios, but growth that is far higher than ours. India had growth of over five per cent in the last quarter of 2011 alone. The UK economy will have zero or negative growth this year, and that is the most optimistic of forecasts. India's economy – her GDP – has grown by over sixty per cent in the past two years, whereas the UK economy grew by 1.9 per cent over the same period. Brazil has grown by 7.2 per cent over the same period, and although this is not as dramatic as India, this is still almost four times faster growth than in the UK.

What is the difference here? Both Brazil and India are benefitting from government-supported growth. At the very least, you can say that neither country is experiencing austerity measures on the basis of the size of their debt. Regardless, what is obvious is that countries like India and Brazil are catching us up – or that we are falling behind.

Keeping with the theme, Japan has a debt level of 228 per cent and rising, yet it is not a country that is on the brink of bankruptcy. 'Japan is the third largest economy in the world. It's a huge customer for Britain's goods. It's also a massive investor back into Britain,' David Cameron commended Japan to us on his visit there in April 2012.[40] He didn't lecture about their unsustainable level of debt. And the facts seem to bear out the rosy picture the Prime Minister is painting of a country with 228 per cent level of debt. Unemployment in Japan is 4.6 per cent, ours is 8.2 per cent, and while their growth is two per cent, ours is flat.

Another interesting case is Canada. In 1994 the government decided on an experiment, setting the country on an austerity spiral. Prime minister Jean Chretien presented what was called his 'bloodbath budget' in an effort to deal with a nine per cent government deficit. He decided to cut it through a combination of eighty per cent spending cuts and twenty per cent tax increases. The effect was a reduction in government spending of twenty per cent. Sound familiar? It should do. This is the model for the coalition government's current economic policy:

'Examples like Sweden and Canada in the past, are so important,' Osborne confirmed. Never mind that the austerity budgets in Canada were conducted against a growing world economy, or that the neighbouring economy of the USA in particular was booming, whereas ours is set against a recession in our key markets.

Yet after going through austerity budgets, and reducing public spending to below forty per cent of GDP, Canada still has a public debt that is higher than the UK – eighty-five per cent. There is no talk of Canada being on the brink of bankruptcy or close to losing its credit rating. What is surprising is how stark the data is. It is difficult to interpret the graph of UK national debt in any way, other than to see this period as historically low. But it doesn't fit a debt narrative and is uncomfortable for debt 'moralists' to explain away.

Let's go back to John Mann on the Treasury Select Committee. 'The national debt that we have, is that the highest in our history?'

You can see why George Osborne didn't want to answer the question. 'It is in cash terms,' he told us through gritted teeth. But we know that debt is measured as a percentage of GDP, and it is not only George Osborne who didn't want to talk about that. Where have we seen these simple facts about our debt as presented in this chapter in the press, media, and commentaries, or posed as questions when politicians, economists and commentators talk about debt?

So there you have it. Our debt is very close to the EU limit on debt, and has been throughout the 'debt crisis' until recently. Our debt is historically low and our debt is lower than most of our trading partners. So what about the deficit?

III
Two Sides to Deficit

Every truth has two sides; it is as well to look at both,
before we commit ourselves to either
– Aesop

It is easy to get mixed up between *debt* and *deficit*. Len McCluskey, the general secretary of Unite the Union, did when he was interviewed on the *Today* programme by Evan Davis. He had the audacity to challenge the debt narrative and faced the full forensic scepticism of one of the debt storytellers. Evan took aim and fired.

McCluskey was making the case that our national debt was historically low, and you would have thought that this is such a rare argument to hear on our public airwaves that it would have begged journalistic inquiry and probing. But even if Davis realised this, he seemed more intent on making Len McCluskey look misinformed. We weren't the only ones who noticed; so did *The Guardian*'s Aditya Chakraborrty:

Davis is a proper economist, so he then got cross over McCluskey's claim that the deficit is not high by historic or contemporary standards. Both the annual deficit – as a percentage of GDP – and the country's accumulated historic debt are high, the BBC man insisted, though he admitted he'd only checked the state back to the mid-80s.

We couldn't let that go. We emailed Davis:

Dear Mr Davis,
Listening to your interview with Len McCluskey yesterday,

you appear yet again to have used editorial language and style to dismiss Len McCluskey's claim that national debt is historically low. This shows a difference in interview style and line of questioning from that which is deployed with government ministers, where assertions for example by Michael Howard last week that the £120m per day debt interest payments are solely due to the previous Labour government borrowing, go unchallenged...[41]

But Davis wasn't having it, 'I can't agree,' he began:

1. LM's claim related to the deficit not the debt. The deficit is huge.
2. He switched on to the debt. That is not high by wartime standards, (not remotely) but it is higher than at any time in about half a century. Before that we were paying for the effects of WW2 which cost an order of magnitude more than anything going on at the moment.[42]

We were subject to the same confusion, when we called in to Five Live to speak to Danny Finkelstein, a journalist who has advised Conservative Party leaders John Major and William Hague; he even attended full cabinet when it was discussing political issues. Our question about debt was dismissed as a question about deficit. It wasn't.

Now we know what debt is. It is the total accumulated amount of money that the government owes as a result of its borrowing, as described in the previous chapter. So what, then, is the deficit? Alastair Darling informs us that it is 'the difference between what you spend and what you receive back in tax'.[43] It is a gap that is filled by government borrowing (bonds), which is how the scale of a deficit is measured. The amount the government borrows over the year adds to the previous years' total of borrowing, which is our public debt. So if *debt* were £900bn at the start of a year and the *deficit* for this year is £100bn, then the national debt will grow to £1,000bn.

So we can begin to see that when you consider what the deficit means, you need to consider two sides to this particular equation – income and spend. Income is mainly generated from what the government raises in taxes; spending is on the NHS, pensions, welfare, defence and so forth – public services. You wouldn't think there were two sides to the deficit the way it is discussed in the political arena though, where the majority of comments and analysis focus on government spending. But does government spend too much – or take in too little?

The main solution posited by our political leaders from all parties, to the deficit and our growing debt, is cuts – we spend 'too much'. It is almost turned into a science.

If you look internationally at when countries have had to deal with horrendous budget deficits, like the one that we were left by Labour, the international evidence shows that the 80/20 split is about the right proportion.[44]

David Cameron called this a 'gold standard', but actually it was Canada's proposed solution to deficit reduction that he decided to adopt. 'I and my colleagues,' (that includes Vince Cable and his fellow Liberal Democrat members of the government) 'going back to the party conference last year [2009] argued that there had to be major cuts.' So why do we need to have the cuts again, Vince? 'Given the growing anxiety about sovereign risks, governments have got to respond to it.'[45] Remember that Alastair Darling had already told us in an interview with Nick Robinson of the BBC on 25 March that the cuts would be 'deeper and tougher' than Margaret Thatcher's in the 1980s.

All of these arguments have the implicit and explicit assumption that the deficit was caused by or is linked to government spending which, supposedly, has been and is too high. But, as there are two sides to the deficit calculation, could it not be that the income coming into government was too low? We'll look at that shortly. But Osborne and others have introduced another aspect to deficit: 'As I have made clear, our aim will be to eliminate the bulk of the structural current budget deficit over a Parliament.'[46] *The Guardian* reported that Vince Cable had claimed that 'it was realistic for the coalition to eradicate the structural deficit by the end of this parliament, adding 'our credibility hinges on it'.[47]

So is the deficit now 'structural', and if so, what does that mean? Well, 'a structural deficit is when a budget deficit persists for some time.'[48] Or, as Alastair Darling said, it is that bit of the deficit that 'is not merely the result of economic ups and downs'.[49] Could it not be made a little clearer? 'The portion of a country's budget deficit that is not the result of changes in the economic cycle. The *structural deficit* will exist even when the economy is at the peak of the cycle.'[50] In other words, it is that bit of the deficit that will still be there even when the economy is functioning normally, i.e. not in recession. But to calculate the 'structural deficit' you would need to forecast what the government income and expenditure will be when the economy is performing normally. And you would also need to forecast when the economy will be performing normally. What *is* 'normal'?

This calculation, then, is based on a forecast of what the economy will be years in advance, based on all kinds of assumptions. The calculation depends on whether a government decides to increase or reduce taxation and spending, and is predicated on a forecast of tax revenue when an economy starts to grow. In fact, there are so many variables to consider before a structural deficit can be determined that the concept is not universally accepted; in other words, 'the idea of a structural deficit serves a political rather than analytical function. It's a pseudo-scientific concept which serves to legitimate what is in fact a pure judgment call – that borrowing needs cutting.'[51]

The Treasury itself will come up with a calculation of structural deficit, usually as a percentage of the total current deficit, but even the Treasury considers that calculating the structural deficit 'remains subject to significant uncertainty'.[52] Alastair Darling himself had to admit that 'trying to calculate what is "structural" in the deficit and what is temporary can take years to work out'.[53] It is a long-term calculation, and as John Maynard Keynes said, 'In the long run we are all dead.'[54]

So it looks for all the world like a red herring, as the calculation of deficit still comes down to a balance between income and expenditure. When commentators, economists and politicians talk about 'structural' deficit, what they are often really talking about is government spending. These are ultimately political decisions about how much and on what we want spend from the public purse and from where the money will come to pay for it.

So what is the level of deficit? By the end of March 2012 it was £127bn, or around 8.4 per cent of our GDP. This is a reduction in the deficit from the peak of the recession, when it was £145bn. Deficit is talked about in such alarmist terms you would think that there had never been a deficit before. But is that correct? It is worth remembering that before we entered the recession the deficit was running consistently at around 2 to 2.5 per cent of GDP. In 2006 the deficit was around £33bn and in 2008 it was £37.8bn. The EU, in the Growth and Stability Pact, as it did with national debt, set an annual deficit level or government borrowing level of three per cent of GDP. Up to the start of the recession in 2008, the deficit was within this level. Since the recession and the need for greater government borrowing, countries across the EU have smashed this deficit ceiling. By 2009 France was running a deficit of 7.5 per cent, Greece 12.7 per cent, [55] Italy 5.3 per cent and even Germany had crept over the limit to 3.2 per cent.

The fact is that governments always borrow, which means there is almost always a deficit. As the reader will recall from the last chapter, national debt started in 1692 at £1m and it is now £1,006 bn, which tells us that debt has been rising for most, if not all, governments every year. So deficit is far from being a new phenomenon. In fact, even if you take the period from 1982 to 2012, you will see that in eighteen years of Conservative government there were only two years when it did not run a deficit. The last Labour government (1997–2010) ran a deficit for nine of its thirteen years in power. So government tends to borrow, and there are good reasons for it; the main one is to plug the gap between income and expenditure in order to meet cash flow commitments.

The other reason is to support economic development. Think of a road haulage company; the better the roads are, the quicker and more cheaply across the country its goods will move. The company cannot afford (and is not inclined to pay for) road improvements, but the government can afford it, and can do it. It may have to borrow money to finance such road building, but this increased capacity can increase growth and GDP – at which point the money is recouped through more tax income. And government can borrow a lot more cheaply than haulage companies. It is, in that sense, more efficient for the government to owe money than for private enterprise to do so.

So deficit isn't all bad. We can assume that the level of deficit and the length of time for which a government runs a high deficit *depend* on what upper limit of public debt an economy can tolerate. The counter argument to the debt storytellers is that we can sustain our level of debt, at least for a while. Remember: we sustained more than 100 per cent debt to GDP for more than twenty years after the war; Japan is doing so now.

Before we move on to look at other plausible causes of the deficit and alternative solutions to closing it, it is useful to look at what government spends and from where it gets its income.

Government Spending

Government spends most of its money in eleven general areas of expenditure. Just to explain, 'public sector interest' is what the government pays to service its borrowing, and they are like monthly repayments on a mortgage or loan. These are the interest payments on the bonds that were discussed earlier.

Pensions payments were moved from 'Social Security' to 'Public Pension' in the 1990s, which is why both budget headings change over that period. Otherwise, if you compare the percentages or proportions of what government decides to spend its money on, it stays fairly consistent over the years.

Although public spending increases year on year, so does the level of GDP, but despite this the percentage of GDP spent on the public sector does change. These are, quite rightly, political decisions and depend on what different Conservative or Labour governments decide are their priorities – remember Tony Blair pouring extra money into the NHS? We've taken four dates to test this out, which mark the end of periods of Labour or Conservative government. We have chosen these so that we can reflect on how political decisions change public spending. The years are: 1979, after the Wilson/Heath/Callaghan Labour governments; 1997 after the Thatcher/Major Conservative governments; and 2010, after the last Labour government. We have also chosen 1961, mainly because this is the year one of us was born and it gives some historical perspective.

GDP in 1961 was about £27bn, whereas in 2012 it is about £1,552 bn. But, as GDP increases, so does government spending. Although the percentages of spend for each area of expenditure stay pretty consistent throughout this period, the total level of public spending as a percentage of GDP has changed a lot from 1961 to 2012. In 1961 we spent 37.6 per cent of our GDP on the public sector, but it rose to 42.75 per cent by 1979, when the Thatcher Conservative government came to power. By the time Labour won an election in 1997 the level of public spending as a percentage of GDP had fallen back to 37.63 per cent. The last Labour government increased public spending to just under forty per cent of GDP. This increased to forty-five per cent in 2010, though this percentage increase was not so much due to political decisions, but because spending had stayed consistent, while GDP had fallen as a result of the recession. But more of that later, when we deal with 'overspending'.

Income

What about the income side of the deficit equation? As an example, the overall tax revenue for government in 2011–2 was £588bn. This is made up of all sorts of income including income tax, national insurance, VAT, excise duty and inheritance tax.[56] Income tax accounts for about twenty-six per cent of total tax receipts, or around £156.6bn. This is the main progressive tax that we have in the UK, which means that the more you earn the more you pay; the top ten per cent of earners pay fifty-five per cent of all income tax. But that has to be balanced against the top ten per cent earning thirty-five per cent of all income. That is a progressive tax system in operation – wealth distribution.

In fact from the table below, you can see that the top one per cent of income earners in our country pay almost twenty-five per cent of the total income tax.

Top earner's tax burden
How income tax paid varies with level of income

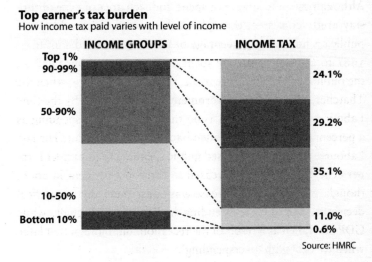

Source: HMRC

But that is only a quarter of the whole tax revenue the government takes as income. Everyone pays the same rate of National Insurance, VAT, fuel, alcohol and tobacco duties, regardless of how much they earn. As this is taxation that takes no account of income, it is regressive taxation, because people on low incomes pay a higher proportion of their income in tax than people on high incomes – this is the opposite of wealth distribution. More than forty-six per cent of tax is paid this way. The rest of taxation is paid by companies, and as council tax to local authorities.

It is this level of detail of spending and income that Chancellors of the Exchequer consider when they are planning their annual budget. They are all subject to change by Chancellors, which is why many of the decisions over spending are clearly political. For example, what should the highest rate of tax be, how much should companies pay in tax or how much should we spend on welfare benefits or pensions? So not only are there two sides to the deficit equation – spending and income – but there are multiple considerations within each side of this equation. How a Government decides what to tax and spend is what is known as fiscal policy.

The Deficit was Caused by Overspending

So now we know there are two sides to the deficit equation, it makes it easier to make sense of the explanations we have been given for why it has arisen in the UK in the first place. The most blatant economic myth would have us believe that the deficit has been caused by overspending by the last Labour government. Even Lord Desai, a Labour candidate for speaker of the House of Lords, has perpetuated this fiction:

> Unlike previous recessions, which were caused by lack of effective demand – the standard Keynesian case – it was due to overspending on the part of households and governments.[57]

Ben Chu, the economics editor at the *Independent* put this nicely into context:

> There is a dividing line in British politics. It runs between those who believe that 2008 was a crisis brought about by rampant financial markets and those who think it was a crisis of excessive government spending. The line runs through parties as well as between them.[58]

And that is why this government believes that 'the bulk of the reduction must come from lower spending rather than higher taxes'.[59] But it is not just the spending that George Osborne was getting at when he announced his intention to 'bring the years of ever-rising borrowing to an end'.[60] Osborne is trying to convince us of a link between what he suggests is 'ever-rising borrowing', and 'ever-rising spending'. But is there?

Earlier we learned that public spending as a proportion of GDP rose under the last Labour government from 37.63 per cent in 1997 to just under forty per cent of GDP by 2008. But did this lead to 'rising borrowing'?

Let's look at the borrowing graph again. The line shows government deficit and the blue bars show the level of borrowing that the governments needed to finance the deficit. The Office of National Statistics has done this for us, calculating deficit and borrowing as a percentage of GDP so that we can make like-for-like comparisons. The Credit Crunch and subsequent financial crisis hit in 2008, so if we are looking for the cause of the increase in the deficit we need to use the figures for deficit and borrowing prior to 2008.

The period from 1982–1997 included fifteen out of the last eighteen years of Conservative government and the borrowing ranged from almost negative two per cent to just under eight per cent of GDP; under Labour governments the borrowing figures from 1997–2008 never went higher than four per cent. For most of the period of each government, it is clear from this graph that Conservative governments borrowed *more* than Labour governments.

When the bars go under zero, that means the government budget was in surplus, and that as a country we were reducing the level of our national debt – paying off more maturing bonds than we were selling. As you can see in the period of Conservative governments there were only two years when this happened –

between 1988 and 1990. This represented less than two per cent of GDP in debt reduction. Whereas the Labour governments paid back debt for three years from 1998 to 2001, which was equivalent to reducing debt by over four per cent of GDP. Alastair Darling put it another way: 'Between 1979 and 1997, the Conservative government borrowed on average 3.4 per cent of national income; between 1997 and 2007, Labour's borrowing averaged 1.2 per cent.'[61]

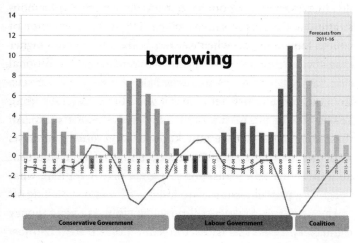

Governments always borrow

Source: Public Finances Databank, ONS

This suggests that spending and borrowing under the last government were not rising or spiralling out of control. In fact, they were lower than they had been in previous governments. That means that the increase in public spending to just under forty per cent of GDP was not matched by ratcheting up public borrowing or 'maxing out our credit card'. In fact, in the period of the early 1980s and 1990s, there was a policy of disinvestment in public services. The Thatcher government came into power under a banner of privatisation of government assets and services. The construction of council housing came to a virtual standstill as private building was prioritised, and there was a lack of investment, indeed cuts, in hospitals, schools, universities and local authorities.

The early 1980s was a period of cuts – but cuts that were explicitly politically motivated to reflect the belief of the government of the day in reducing the level of services provided by the state, to be replaced by private services where possible. It was a dividing line between political parties; there were huge demonstrations and arguments in the media. This is a simplification of course, but at the time when we were borrowing at levels higher than the last Labour government we were earning additional cash (at least £25.6 bn) from the sale of state-owned assets: from the sale of British Telecom (£8.9bn), British Steel (£2.5bn), British Gas (£5bn), BP (£7.25bn) and British Rail (£1.96bn). All these companies that we now know as large private interests were owned by the state at that time. Putting aside the argument about whether nationalisation is a good or a bad thing, what the government did was to earn billions of pounds in selling off these companies, and yet still run a deficit and borrow money to finance it. And this is not to mention that Britain had just started to generate income from the sale of oil found in the North Sea.

North Sea oil income was £11bn per year at its peak in 1985, three per cent of GDP. The reserves are now starting to run out and in 1997 the income was down to £2bn, 0.3 per cent of GDP. By 2010, with the worldwide increase in the price of crude oil, the income was still only £6.4bn, 0.44 per cent of GDP.[62] The point is that if there had not been North Sea oil revenue in the 1980s and the windfall from the sale of nationalised companies, the government may well have had to borrow more money and the deficit could easily have been as high in 1985 as it is today.

Fast-forward to 1997, when the last Labour government came to power. There was very little income from the sale of state assets, the income from North Sea oil had reduced significantly and there was a need to invest in our schools, hospitals, roads and housing. (There is a small caveat here, as a lot of this investment in schools and hospitals has been financed from Private Finance Initiatives.) The Labour government chose to invest as a political priority, yet it borrowed less than in the previous period of Conservative governments to do so. In fact, the country had a long period of economic stability.

Listen to what Mervyn King, the governor of the Bank of England had to say: 'Before the crisis, steady growth with low inflation and high employment was in our grasp.'[63] This is the same governor who helped George Osborne and David Cameron to work up their economic policy prior to the 2010 general election, with an unprecedented programme of public sector cuts. Yet he is being quite clear in saying that the economy 'before the crisis' was doing okay. He is not suggesting that the crisis in 2008 and the resultant increase in the deficit and the increase in borrowing was the fault of previous government spending and borrowing.

So what was the cause of the deficit? Let's go back to Mervyn again: 'The billions spent bailing out the banks and the need for public spending cuts were the fault of the financial services sector.'[64]

If we have been watching BBC News, *Newsnight* and *Question Time* and listening to the *Today* programme we have heard little other than 'It was Labour that got us into this mess'; 'Too much spending'; 'Too much borrowing'; 'On the brink of bankruptcy'. We haven't heard Mervyn King's comments mentioned much, if at all, and certainly not in journalistic questions or economic commentary.

But the deficit is the thing, we are told, that is crippling us. 'Deficit reduction and continuing to ensure economic recovery is the most urgent issue facing Britain,' is the first item in the 2010 Coalition Agreement.[65] And why is that? 'We are paying, at a rate of £120 million a day, £43 billion a year in debt interest.' Osborne introduced this idea to us in 2010 and it has been repeated consistently by Liberal Democrat and Conservative spokespeople ever since. Michael Howard, the former leader of the Conservative Party, and Home Secretary in previous governments, just won't let this go. Whenever he is on BBC 1's *Question Time*, he can't wait to get that fact out. Of course, Vince Cable says it as well, and as if that doesn't make us feel bad enough he goes on to say that 'one pound in every four that they spent – on everything from our pensions to our police to our schools – was borrowed'. David Cameron goes further: 'We're borrowing so much that next year, the government will spend more money on the interest on our debt than on schools.'[66] *Oh my goodness, we are spending more on creating debts for our children than we are on educating them.* But hang on. The debt interest payments we have been making for years and years were almost as high as the entire education budget including universities and colleges in 1961 and 1998. So that also means that as we have a long history of deficit and debt, we have a long history of making interest payments to service the debt.

It is just when you say 'we are spending £120m every day on servicing our debt' that it sounds so big and scary. But how does this compare to previous years and previous governments? We know from the last chapter that interest on our borrowing is not really paid like this. To recap, our borrowing is financed by issuing bonds, which have an annual payment until they mature and are repaid out in full. And remember, bonds issued years ago need repaying today, and we issue new bonds to replace them, if we need to. So interest payments will actually vary through the year, and the £43bn is the annual accumulated figure that the government is paying in debt interest payments. We are not really paying £120m per day – that is just a political device, we would suggest, to create anxiety over debt. We get to this figure by dividing £43bn by 365 days. It is as crude as that. To be pedantic it should be £117.8m per day.

The question is, are these payments high or low, significant or insignificant, different from before or not?

Using debt interest payments as a percentage of GDP we can see that in 2012, £43bn is the equivalent of 2.84 per cent of GDP. Back in 1982, at the peak of government cuts in that year, Thatcher's government was paying the equivalent of 5.15 per cent of GDP. That was the equivalent of paying £174 million pounds a day. And there was no talk in 1982 of the country being on the brink of bankruptcy. In fact, this government and the last one paid less every year in debt interest payments than the previous eighteen years of Conservative governments had done.

Furthermore, prior to the current economic crisis, UK debt interest payments had been running at between £25bn and £30bn for over ten years, when Mervyn King was happy with the condition of our economy. This reflects debt interest payments in every year of every government, going back for as long as you want to look. Even when, after 2008, we needed to borrow such huge amounts to finance our deficit, it only added an additional £13bn per year to our debt interest payments. And as we will see later in the book, £5bn of that is what it is costing us to borrow money to finance the banks.[67]

The argument that our debt interest payments are unsustainable is another myth. In fact, the cost of our borrowing today is low, has been since 1999, and it is perfectly sustainable. Of course we would prefer not to have a high deficit, but for the time being, as a nation, we can afford the annual repayments. The main reason why borrowing was so expensive in the 1980s and 1990s was that the interest the government was paying on the bonds we issued was very high. This was reflected in mortgage payments as well, when the interest rate for mortgages rose to fifteen per cent, not the 4.5 – 6 per cent that it is today. The same is true of government borrowing.

Not only is our borrowing cheap, it is the cheapest that it has ever been. The cost of benchmark five-year government bonds fell to 1.43 per cent, which the *Financial Times* quotes as being the lowest rate of interest since banks started collecting data in 1985, and is most likely the lowest since the 1950s. Ten-year bonds are the lowest since records began in the 1950s. This is how the *Financial Times* puts it:

> Five-year gilt yields fell to 1.43 per cent on Thursday, almost a quarter of a percentage point below those of Germany, which traditionally benefits from much lower interest rate costs. Five-year gilts yields are at their lowest levels since 1985, when banks started collecting the data, and bankers say five-year yields are probably at the lowest since the early 1950s, although they do not have data to back this assertion. Ten-year yields, however, are trading around lows since 1958, which is the furthest back the records of most banks go.[68]

That confirms it. Government borrowing is cheap. And not only is it cheap, but we are borrowing money by issuing bonds that do not have to be repaid for five, ten or even fifteen years. So that begs another question: why do we need to pay off, or even halve, the deficit in four years when we have borrowing that runs for up to fifteen? What's more if we need to we can issue new bonds to replace old ones that extends the period we owe money. So what is the significance of four years? This is not the period of an economic cycle, but four years takes us to

2015, when the next election is. That is more like a political cycle.

What is to stop us using the fact that borrowing is cheap and over a long period of time, to invest in public services, infrastructure projects and the economy, instead of paying for austerity? In fact, the other most recent period we experienced long years of unusually low interest rates (two per cent) was in the period 1932 to 1952, when we fought a world war – the most expensive public sector expenditure ever – and that is when we built a welfare state.[69] That is why – to reiterate – Paul Krugman told us that 'jobs now, deficits later was and is the right strategy'.[70] This runs counter to the debt story, because most politicians, most quoted economists, commentators and journalists do not consider investment in the economy to stimulate growth as an ideologically acceptable option. *Why not?*

IV
What Caused the Deficit?

The relation between what we see and what we know is
never settled. Each evening we see the sun set. We know
that the earth is turning away from it. Yet the knowledge,
the explanation, never quite fits the sight.
– John Berger, *Ways of Seeing*

So if it wasn't overspending that caused the deficit, what was it?
In 2008 the growing tsunami of the home loan crisis in the
United States hit the UK economy with such force that it almost
stunned our financial services into paralysis. Our banks had
bought the mortgages the US financial institutions had given to
people who couldn't afford the repayments. They were nevertheless valued as copper-bottomed investments, even rated AAA by
the corporate credit rating agencies. But as these mortgages were
foreclosing in their millions, these investments became worthless, which meant that our banks couldn't sell the mortgage-
backed investments on. They got stuck with them, and ended up
running out of money.

The result was what become known as the 'Credit Crunch'
(not, you might note, the 'Bank Debacle' – see how the narrative
runs?). While Alastair Darling was meeting with bank chief
executives and buying RBS and Northern Rock on the tax-
payer's behalf, the banks were withdrawing overdrafts and not
lending money to businesses. Mortgages and loans became very
difficult to come by. People stopped spending as much in the
shops, businesses had cash flow problems caused by losing
overdrafts and having no access to loans and were closing or
shrinking. We were shopping less and the result was a shock to
the economy that turned it from a stable growth of three per

cent per year into a slump – or negative growth. In 2007–10 our economy shrank by ten per cent; in other words the GDP fell by ten percent.

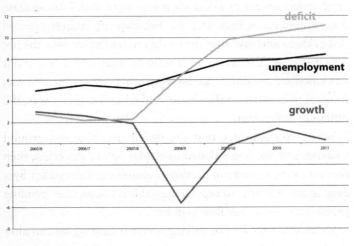

Growth & deficit linked

As you can see from the graph, as the economy slumped, people were being laid off and unemployment increased by sixty-six per cent, from under 1.5m 2007 to around 2.5m in 2010.

That was roughly one million people who were not paying taxes and who started claiming benefits. If you remember, there are two sides to the deficit calculation, so what we experienced was a slump in the amount of income the government received from corporation tax, income tax, VAT and National Insurance, because people were out of work and businesses were closing. Meanwhile, public spending on schools, hospitals and local authorities, etc. remained the same as forecast, and only increased in line with inflation, consistent with increases in previous years. Spending was going ahead as planned; the problem was the drop in income to the government and that is what created the deficit. So it wasn't overspending that caused the deficit, but, rather, insufficient income.

If we look at tax revenue in more detail, we can see that it appears to increase by about six per cent per year. This increase is consistent going back to 1979. But focusing in on the period just prior to and just after the credit crunch, we can see the tax deficit emerge. Tax receipts fell between 2007 and 2010, and if you calculate the difference between what the tax income was forecast to be without the slump, and what it actually was, the difference is £100bn.

When you consider that the deficit in 2010 was around £145bn, and we had a deficit of £30bn before the crisis, then the rest of the deficit can be almost entirely accounted for by a drop in tax receipts. To repeat, then, this is not an overspending problem; this is a cash-flow problem.

So we don't have to be talking about spending, we can alter the focus of deficit reduction to how we can increase income. There is also a difference between *reducing* the deficit and the deficit *reducing*. If a lack of growth can increase a deficit, can growth in the economy reduce the deficit?

The government response to the economic crisis in 2008 and 2009 was to embark on a period of what was called 'fiscal stimulus'. The *Financial Times* Lexicon defines this as: 'government measures, normally involving increased public spending and lower taxation, aimed at giving a positive jolt to economic activity'.[71] And that is what the last Labour government did. In 2008 there was a £20bn injection into the economy, and it seemed to pay off. This was pure Keynesian economics, using the might of the state to step in where the private sector is lacking, to keep money circulating around the economy and keep people in work. Keynes warned against what he called the 'paradox of thrift'. This is where a citizen's natural reaction to economic crisis is to save and not spend. The cumulative effect is a reduction in GDP. Even Adam Smith wrote that 'what is prudence in the conduct of every private family can scarce be folly in that of a great Kingdom'.[72] But Keynes said that government must step in and start spending to keep people employed and to keep the economy functioning.

Gordon Brown seized on this and encouraged European neighbours and the USA to follow suit with their own fiscal stimuli. There were no significant austerity measures; VAT was reduced and investment projects were maintained. As a result our economy came out of the deepest recession since the 1930s in October 2009. Between then and May 2010, our GDP increased by 1.7 per cent. This was a comparable quarterly growth to what we had seen in the UK for years. Remember that the economy grew between two and three per cent per year (an average of 0.75 per cent per quarter) from 1997 to 2008. As a result, unemployment did not rise to the three million mark, as many economists were forecasting, and instead peaked at 2.4 million. The deficit, which was forecast by Alastair Darling to reach £167bn by the end of March 2010, actually came in at £145bn. This is still relatively high, but as a result of pumping money into the economy and keeping people in work as much as possible, the deficit was £22bn less than was forecast. In other words, we borrowed £22bn less than was forecast. When the Coalition government came into power in May 2010, the deficit was actually £30bn lower than was forecast. So if 1.7 per cent growth can have that impact on deficit reduction, what would happen to the deficit if there was three per cent per year growth, without making any cuts whatsoever? Worth thinking about, isn't it?

When the Coalition government came to power in 2010, you would have expected it to have worked up its budget for that and subsequent years, based on the information and forecasts that are publicly available in the Treasury. The tax and spending calculations would presumably have been based on a deficit of £167bn that they thought they would have inherited.

Not only that, but the incoming government received insider assistance from the Governor of the Bank of England. It turns out that the US government cables revealed by Wikileaks included emails from the American ambassador to the UK that had references to Mervyn King having held private meetings with David Cameron and George Osborne as they prepared their economic policy for the 2010 general election. The ambassador goes on to report that King was urging the Conservatives to draw up a detailed plan to reduce the deficit.[73] This is unprecedented. Professor Danny Blanchflower, who was a member of the Bank of England Monetary Policy Committee was astonished. 'He [King] has now committed the unforgivable sin of compromising the independence of the Bank of England by involving himself in the economic policy of the Coalition. He is expected to be politically neutral but has shown himself to be politically biased and as a result is now in an untenable position.'[74]

This is a nuanced point, but a significant one. The Bank of England, through its control of interest rates, is responsible for monetary policy, which means the amount of money circulating in the economy and how much money costs to lend and borrow. This function of the bank is independent of government and has no role in fiscal policy, and is not influenced by decisions over public spending and taxation. So for the governor of the Bank of England to be advising on government economic policy is inappropriate and quite possibly unconstitutional.

But for our purposes, however inappropriate it was, it shows how much information on the country's finances the incoming Coalition government was privy to. Listen to what Vince Cable had to say:

I received unequivocal advice from top government economic officials and the Bank of England that any incoming government needed to act immediately to shore up confidence and reduce the risk of contagion.[75]

This is the partial view of Mervyn King – what business is it of his to decide that the spending cuts were the best way to reduce the deficit? That is a political decision.

So given that the deficit was £30bn lower than expected and the incoming economics team had unprecedented access to Treasury data, why was it that the first thing that the new Chancellor of the Exchequer did was to make a cut in the 2010–11 financial year of £6bn? Why was that needed if the starting point for the Coalition government budget was a lower deficit than expected? That smacks of ideological rather than economics driven policy, doesn't it?

Let's look a little closer at the income side of the deficit equation. Tax has changed significantly over the past forty years. In 1975 the high rate of tax was eighty-three per cent and the basic rate was thirty-three per cent. There wasn't a standard shopping tax, as there is now, but a purchase tax that was only levied on certain goods, usually luxury items. Since 1975 the tax system has been transformed. The high rate of tax has been reduced to forty per cent, although it was temporarily increased to fifty per cent in 2010 and is set to reduce to forty-five per cent in 2013. The basic rate of tax has gone down to twenty per cent. At the same time, the patchy purchase tax was replaced with VAT in 1973. Initially this was introduced at ten per cent and reduced to eight per cent the following year. In 1979 it was raised to fifteen per cent and in 1990 to 17.5 per cent. In 2010 it was raised to the same level as the basic rate of tax – twenty per cent.

This change in tax policy, as we explained earlier, represents a shift from *progressive* taxation based on what we earn, to *regressive* taxation based on what we spend – from taxation to redistribute wealth fairly to taxation to shift the burden to the lower paid. Not surprisingly, this has meant that over exactly the same period the UK has become a much more unequal society.

The Gini coefficient, a World Bank standard measurement tool of inequality, records how much citizens have to spend after deducting their household costs. It measures disposable income. Since the 1970s the Gini coefficient shows an increasing gap between the poor and the well off to the point that 'income inequality in the UK is now higher than at any previous time in the last thirty years'. As if that wasn't bad enough, the UN published its Human Development Report in December 2010[76] confirming that the UK has become the most unequal society in the western, developed world. We ranked twenty-sixth in the Human Development Index, behind the USA, Belgium, Luxembourg, Germany, France and all our European and trading partners. That is even before the austerity package of cuts to welfare benefits and tax credits currently being dispensed have taken hold. UNICEF has estimated that as a result of these cuts, child poverty will return to pre-1997 levels. And this comes after a survey by UNICEF that found our children have the lowest well-being in the developed world[77]. Even the Organisation for Economic Co-operation and Development recorded that the UK is the most unequal society in the developed, industrialised world.

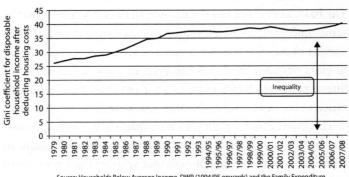

Source: Households Below Average Income. DWP (1994/95 onwards) and the Family Expenditure Survey (earlier years) obtained via data published by the IFS: UK: updated Aug 2009

Apart from the social, health and educational issues that inequality creates in society, what this tells us is that people on high incomes have more disposable income now than they did in 1975. And that means they have more capacity to pay tax than they do now. This has not gone unnoticed, even though it is not part of our political narrative.

HMRC estimates what it calls the 'tax gap' every year. This is a combination of:

- unpaid taxes
- tax evasion, where people break the law and don't declare the tax they owe
- tax avoidance where people and companies used loopholes in tax law to get round paying the tax expected of them

The latest figures prior to this book going to print are for 2009–10, with HMRC telling us that 'overall the total tax gap is estimated to be £35 billion in 2009–10'. Vodafone alone negotiated a reduction in its £8bn tax bill in 2010 to just £1.25bn,[78] and remarkably paid zero corporation tax in 2011.[79] Lloyds Bank made £2.2bn of profit in 2010 and also paid zero corporation tax.[80] We also know that Barclays Bank was engaged in arranging tax avoidance schemes for its clients that in themselves could amount to billions of pounds of unpaid tax.[81]

Philip Green, a retail billionaire recently employed as an efficiency advisor to the Coalition government, is perhaps the most public face of alleged tax avoidance. Mr Green is associated with the growth of the Arcadia group of businesses, which we know on the high street as Burtons, Top Shop, Dorothy Perkins and Miss Selfridge. *The Guardian* tells us that it was Mrs and not Mr Green, who was paid the biggest known dividend payment in history of £1.25bn, 'the record-breaking payment went to his wife, Tina, who lives in Monaco and is the direct owner of Arcadia. Because of this arrangement no UK income tax was due on the gain.' Monaco is an offshore tax haven. The tax payable on that amount is £285m.[82] For this reason alone it might be prudent for Philip not to be too vocal about the deficit.

Tax avoidance measures are not just about wealthy people. Through personal experience we have come across agency staff working in the NHS who have been given a company and an offshore account through which their UK earnings are paid, so that they do not pay tax.

That is why UK Uncut, Tax Research UK (an economics blog on tax and economics) and the TUC estimate that the tax gap could be as high as £120bn per year. Taking all the above into account, that is not that difficult to believe. When you consider that the current deficit for 2011–12 is £127bn, it rather puts the deficit into a different perspective. The TUC estimates that tax avoidance alone from individuals and from the 700 largest corporations represents '£13 billion per annum'.[83]

Tax avoidance has particular significance for the public sector. Until the early 1980s, almost 100 per cent of public services were delivered by publicly employed staff. That meant that public money paid public sector staff, who returned the tax element of their income back to the Treasury. Since the 1980s there has been an increasing drive to outsource public sector services to private companies.

How does this affect tax revenue? Private companies can bring their tax avoidance measures with them when they operate in the public sector, generating profit and offsetting costs. It stands to reason then that private companies will pay less tax than if the service were delivered solely by employed public servants. In the past twenty years the outsourcing of public services to private companies has increased from close to zero to around twenty per cent of public sector spending. Companies such as Tribal, G4S, A4E, Ingeus Deloitte and Capita have become synonymous with the delivery of public services. For example, the Work Programme is a tendered service run by private companies. They have replaced the Job Centre as the agencies working with long term unemployed, amounting to the creation of a privatised employment support programme.

To get a sense of the scale of this, if public spending on services is around £340bn, then 24 per cent of that, £82bn of public services, is outsourced to private companies[84]. The average profit of these companies is five per cent of turnover, which means that around £4.1bn of that spending may not be coming back into the Treasury. At the very least does this not suggest that if there was £4.1bn that did not need to be spent on delivery it could come back to the Treasury or it should have been returned through income or corporation tax? It may be more than that when you take account of book-keeping measures for expenditure (depreciation, costs of the business as a whole rather than the contract, etc). So political decisions to outsource public sector delivery to the private sector has a cost in a reduction in income through taxation to the Treasury.

As we learned earlier we have been in high debt before. At the end of the Second World War, our reserves had gone into the war effort, the government had run up a high deficit and debt was 238 per cent of GDP. But the government had a vision to create a welfare state, build council houses and establish the National Health Service. This all needed money, so on 15 July 1945 the United Kingdom negotiated from the United States a loan equivalent in today's money to £56bn, at two per cent interest. This loan took over sixty years to repay, the final instalment being made on 29 December 2006. The loan from the USA was essential to free up money for the government to invest in welfare reform – schools, hospitals and housing. This is a legacy that we live with today. It's an obvious question isn't it, to ask, 'If we did it then, why can't we do it now?'

Let's contemplate a hypothetical scenario. The government currently pays interest of 2.43 per cent on fifteen-year loans, so if we borrowed £1bn it would cost us £24.3m in repayments per year. If this loan were invested in building social housing, which in the north-west would cost £120,000 each, we could build 8,330 houses. If the houses were let at an affordable rent (this is a level between social housing rent and market rent), the average return would be £5,500 per house per year. Multiply that by 8,330 houses and that is an annual return of £45.8m per year. That is a surplus of £21.5m per year or £322.5m over fifteen years. But when you add inflation of a conservative two per cent per year, then £1bn devalues by two per cent per year, so that in fifteen years' time it is worth at least thirty per cent less than it is today. We would repay the equivalent of £666m, not £1bn.

But if we are taking people off benefits to build these houses, then there is an additional benefit to government. Let's assume the average total benefit receipt of an individual is £100 per week (Job Seekers' Allowance and Housing Benefit), the equivalent of £5,200 per year. If the average wage is £22,000 then the same person will now pay about £3,500 in tax and NI, with a benefit to the public purse of about £8,700 per year. If there were 500 people like this, it would bring in an additional £4.35m per year. They then spend money on goods and services, the suppliers of which would also benefit from additional income and, therefore, pay a little more tax.

Furthermore, a whole range of suppliers would get additional income from contracts generated by supplying materials for the new houses. This increases their company profits with additional corporation and self-assessment tax to pay. The £1bn is going around and around the economy – 'multiplying', in Keynes' terms. If we now add to that the value of new revenue income to the government from taxes of the people employed to build the houses and the saving from not having to pay out welfare benefits, then the dividend to the GDP of the investment increases further.

There are lots of other options that some have suggested. We could have a national investment bank that finances the renewables industry or a green car manufacturer, or big infrastructure projects. All of these have a pay-back to the public purse through income tax, corporation tax, a straight return on investment and the increase in money circulating around the economy.

The benefits of public investment to the economy and the Treasury are huge, hence Keynes' facetious suggestion that

> if the Treasury were to fill old bottles with banknotes, bury them at suitable depths in disused coalmines which are then filled up to the surface with town rubbish, and leave it to private enterprise on well-tried principles of laissez-faire to dig the notes up again (the right to do so being obtained, of course, by tendering for leases of the note-bearing territory), there need be no more unemployment and, with the help of the repercussions, the real income of the community, and its capital wealth also, would probably become a good deal greater than it actually is. It would, indeed, be more sensible to build houses and the like; but if there are political and practical difficulties in the way of this, the above would be better than nothing.[85]

Employment is the key to deficit reduction. It is no surprise that the net effect of public sector cuts has been less money in the economy; tax revenue remains flat, and the deficit remains stubbornly the same. Ireland, Greece and the UK are all experiencing this. Our government is now borrowing £150bn more than was forecast in 2010 – forty-five per cent more than borrowing was forecast to be under an austerity regime.

The UK could introduce a financial transaction ('Robin Hood') tax. Sales of shares and bonds would be taxed at a rate of 0.1 per cent and derivative contracts (investments) at a rate of 0.01 per cent. When you consider that the level of transactions in the City of London is £600 trillion per year, this has the potential of raising at least £30bn per year in additional taxation. Already introduced in many European countries, the impact this would have on deficit reduction is obvious.

So this is not just a choice, as the BBC would lead us to believe, between taxation, cuts and timing. There is also borrowing, investment and return. But how often does that get discussed?

V

The Banks

While stand the banks of England, England stands.
When fall the banks of England, England falls.
– Mary Poppins

Mr Dawes, owner of the Dawes Tomes Mousley Grubbs Fidelity Fiduciary Bank, is surrounded by his fellow directors, as much to catch him if he topples over as to show deference to the man. They wear black ties, nestling in white wing-collared shirts and pin-striped trousers, and stand bolt upright as their lofty position in the bank warrants. Mr Dawes is old, and uses his walking stick as a pivot, as he almost spins right around on its axis. He is staring down at young Michael Banks. Michael can't be more than eleven years old. His father has brought him to the bank to open an account with the tuppence he is holding in his hand. But Michael doesn't want to open a bank account; he wants to use the money to feed the birds, the way Mary Poppins has taught him and his sister, Jane. He doesn't want to give it to Mr Dawes.

Michael's father, Mr Banks, works for Mr Dawes and although he is torn between his responsibility to his employer and his duty to his children, he is coming down on Mr Dawes' side.

'Now Michael,' he begins, 'when you deposit tuppence in a bank account, soon you'll see that it blooms into credit of a generous amount. Semi-annually.'[86] Michael and Jane look quite bemused, incredulous. What is their father talking about?

Mr Dawes takes over, 'And you'll achieve that sense of stature, as your influence expands to the high financial strata that established credit now commands. You can purchase first and second trust deeds. Think of the foreclosures! Bonds, chattels, dividends, shares! Bankruptcies, debtor sales, opportunities! All manner of private enterprise. Shipyards, the mercantile, collieries, tanneries.'

Michael and Jane are being backed into a corner as Mr Dawes, the directors and Mr Banks press closer and closer to them, 'Incorporations, amalgamations. Banks!'[87] With the children cornered, Dawes summons up all the pomposity and majesty he can muster, 'while stand the banks of England, England stands. When fall the banks of England, England falls.' Mary Poppins would not have approved.

You could imagine similar conversations taking place between Alistair Darling, then Chancellor of the Exchequer in the Labour government, the Governor of the Bank of England and the Chief Executives of our banks, who were facing meltdown in 2007. Reading Darling's recollections from those meetings and listening to the commentaries at the time, it was clearly the falls of the banks of England causing England to fall that was uppermost in their minds. 'I [Darling] rang Nick Macpherson at the Treasury and told him his hour had come. He was to tell Mervyn King to put as much money into RBS as was necessary to keep it afloat that day. We would stand behind the Bank, even if it meant using every last penny we had. If RBS closed its doors, the banking system would freeze, not just in the UK but around the world.'[88]

So not only would England fall, but the whole world would. And there you have it – the aloof, foreboding authority of banks. Over the past 4 years, we have seen more pictures of bankers than we can ever remember. They were forced out of their offices and into the limelight to give evidence to the Treasury Select Committee, images of them running into crisis meetings with ministers on the front pages of our newspapers.

These are powerful people. They embody globalisation, as they sit atop businesses that have turnovers of billions of pounds and dollars, trading all over the world. They hold economic authority over world business and are too big and too fundamental to a functioning economy to fail. Or so they tell us. These are intimidating people, with the power to shock and awe. What must it be like to deal with them, let alone challenge them? And what happens if they are invited into government and how might their authority influence decision-making?

In recent years, the most senior officers of the largest financial institutions in the world have been entering the government of the USA, directly influencing and managing fiscal and monetary policy. Henry Merritt 'Hank' Paulson, Treasury Secretary (equivalent to the Chancellor of the Exchequer) during the banking crisis in 2006, had been CEO of Goldman Sachs, one of the biggest financial institutions in the world. Robert Rubin, Treasury Secretary 1995–9, had also been CEO of Goldman Sachs. Tim Geithner, appointed Treasury Secretary in 2009, was president of the Federal Reserve Bank of New York. And the Daddy of them all, Alan Greenspan who was the longest serving Chair of the Federal Reserve (equivalent to Mervyn King) had previously been the managing director at the Wall Street investment bank Brown Brothers Harriman. The list is even bigger when those on the Federal Reserve Board and less senior positions in the USA Treasury are taken into consideration.

Michael Moore, in his film on the Credit Crunch called *Capitalism: a Love Story*, went so far as to say that the infiltration of bank executives – especially those from Goldman Sachs – into the US government was enough to be called a 'financial coup d'etat'. In a particularly poignant moment in the film, a congresswoman who had responsibility for trying (unsuccessfully) to trace what happened to bank bail-out money in the USA reluctantly agrees with Michael Moore that a coup has taken place. But the Goldman Sachs footprint in government goes far deeper.

So, back to our story. At the point when the US banks and AIG were teetering on the verge of bankruptcy, 'Hank' Paulson, US Treasury Secretary, pushed hard for a huge bank bailout. He was at President Bush's right hand, pushing for the government to make the decision to pay up. 'Paulson is spearheading an unprecedented global change as the Bush administration point man for the proposed $700 billion bailout of the U.S. financial industry,'[89] reported *USA Today*. Although the money was lent to the insurance company AIG, Goldman Sachs, the company Paulson used to run, benefited from billions of dollars to compensate them from having a load of worthless investments. Isn't that a conflict of interest?

Alistair Darling was not free of advice from people steeped in the finance industry either. Paul Myners, appointed as the Financial Service Secretary, had been Chief Executive of the Pension Fund for the Gartmore Group, a director of NatWest, and a member of the board of the investment fund RIT Capital Partners. Lady Shrita Vadera was a Minister in the Department for Business, Enterprise and Regulatory Reform in 2008 and came from a career at the investment bank UBS Warsburg. The other key member of the advisory team was Mervyn King, Governor of the Bank of England. So Alistair Darling was surrounded by advisors from the financial services industry. Did that play a role in their objectivity? Who can tell?

Alistair Darling was also working closely with the USA Treasury Secretary, and what did he think about that? 'Hank Paulson, having worked in financial markets, knew what needed to be done.'[90] In fact Alistair quite liked him, 'I warmed to Hank, a bluff amiable man, who was open and direct... the two of us remained in close touch over the next two fraught years until he left office.'[91] Paulson was known as the 'Hammer' in

American financial circles, because of his ruthless, single-minded approach to getting his own way. He certainly hammered through the $700bn US government financial rescue package that benefited his former company by billions of dollars. At the same time we thought in 2008, mainly because we were told, that in the heat of the banking crisis it was reasonable to save the banks. We bought into the idea that if we didn't bail out RBS, then the whole banking system would collapse. We were as spooked as Darling seemed to be – the rabbit caught in the banker's headlights.

Iceland, which incredibly was at the heart of this crisis, had three very large banks that were as bloated and over-leveraged as ours from international investments, deposits and interbank loans. Between them they had debts that were worth ten times the GDP of Iceland. When the credit crunch hit and their banks became insolvent, by popular demand, Kaupthing, Glitnir and Landsbanki banks were allowed to close. Did the country collapse? Did its banking industry collapse? Well no. In fact the government prioritised the ordinary person in the street over the international pension funds and financial institutions.

> Iceland tore up the traditional rulebook. First, retail depositors were given priority over bondholders. Then, alongside the deposits, all domestic assets were transferred to new banks at 'fair value' – the shrunken, market price of the debt. The new banks, recapitalised by the state, took over the vital payments system that kept the wheels of the economy turning.[92]

The government – under pressure from rioting and demonstrating Icelandic citizens – looked after its own people: 'the Icelandic government then took unorthodox measures to alleviate the debt burden on households. Banks were made to accept reductions in mortgage interest payments of up to forty per cent, while the most distressed households had some of their debt written off.'93

Can you imagine Myners, Paulson, King and Vadera having that kind of conversation with the CEOs of RBS, HBOS, Lloyds and Barclays? Was anyone concerned with devising measures to alleviate the rising personal debt, which stood at £1,443bn in 2008? This is an average of £57,950 for each and every household. And this is a debt on each household, unlike government debt. It is ironic that ministers and commentators are appalled at the cost of public debt, but have begun no initiatives to relieve mortgage and credit card debt. In fact, for most homeowners, even though the Bank of England interest rate is 0.5 per cent, and the banks are getting cheap money from the Bank, mortgage interest rates are in excess of four per cent. No reduction there then. No thought for what is now called the 'squeezed middle'. Why not?

Of the $700bn that the United States government pumped into the banks in 2008, not one cent supported people who were losing their homes. Yet the fact that people were losing their homes was the cause of the crisis. Wouldn't giving them money, or insisting the banks reduce the interest they were charging, have stopped the mass foreclosures, retained a value in the housing market and protected the assets of the banks anyway? Hank Paulson seemingly was more interested in saving the banks.

Barry was living in Moscow when the banking system froze in 1998. The Russian banks had borrowed money – lots of it – from foreign banks in dollar currency, and because the Rouble wasn't (and still isn't) an internationally tradeable currency, the repayments had to be paid in dollars. The banks in turn lent the money they had borrowed at high rates of interest to local entrepreneurs, who were making so much profit from buying up businesses and resources that they could afford the high interest rates and repayments.

This was all fine until the rouble fell in value, which meant that it cost a lot more for the banks to buy the dollars to meet the repayments on their interbank loans. In the end the amount of dollars that the banks had to find each month was too great, and the system collapsed. Overnight the banks froze accounts. No one could get their money in or out. This went on for weeks as people didn't get paid, businesses stopped paying each other and people lost money they had on deposit. There were crisis talks with the government, the Russian banks, who decided to default on their interbank loans with foreign banks and then only give people about ten per cent of the value of the money they previously held in their accounts.

Joerg, a friend of Barry's and the former director of the publishing company where he was clinging on to his job, lost over $50,000. People struggled, but stoically accepted it, because that is the way Russian governments behave towards their people. It was unpleasant, but the country didn't collapse, neither did the banks. Russia, like Iceland, is now a growing economy.

But when our government was discussing what to do with the banks, there was only one story in town. We were told we needed to support the banks – otherwise the UK and the world financial system would freeze. Would the banking system have collapsed if we had let all the worthless bank investments of RBS go, but kept all the current, deposit accounts and mortgages? It worked in Iceland and Russia (to a lesser extent), but who presented us with that option in the UK?

Let's recap on how the banks actually did to get into this mess in the first place. As we all know now, the government has bailed out the banks and there are public sector spending cuts. Mervyn King told us in his evidence to the Treasury Select Committee in February 2012 that '...the billions spent bailing out the banks and the need for public spending cuts were the fault of the financial services sector'.[94] But what lay at the very root of the banking crisis and why do we need to bail out the banks? What do we mean when we say we have to re-capitalise the banks? Where has the money gone that the banks have been lent anyway? In other words, what went wrong?

It all boils down to the those 'first and second trust deeds' that Mr Dawes was tempting young Michael Banks with, or as we call them now, mortgage-backed securities – those bank investments that in effect brought banks to bankruptcy. You also get the sense that the conversations about bank bailouts were fuelled by the pomposity embedded in the 'stature' and 'high financial strata' of the bankers, who could not contemplate the banks closing and convinced almost all of us that banks were institutions to be trusted. We saw this in the full glare of the Parliamentary spotlight, when Bob Diamond, the former Chief Executive of Barclays Bank, sat in front of the Treasury Select Committee in 2011 to tell us that it was time to draw a line under all the criticism and vilification that the banks had received over the previous three years. You could tell that he had felt bankers had been treated unjustly and he was waiting for the opportunity to make his point publicly. 'There was a period of remorse and apology for banks. I think that period needs to be over,'[95] he told us. Eighteen months later he had resigned over lying about the interbank borrowing rates and the Libor rate. He apologised.

To start this, we need to understand how banks and money work, and that starts with getting to grips with how banks can lend out more money than they have on deposit. This is what is called the bank liquidity ratio. It's not nearly as complicated as it seems – it's actually rather simple, and it is based on the simple idea that people will not withdraw all the money they need in cash at any one time.

Let's start from the moment when a bank first opens. You go in and open an account. You put £100 into it. The bank holds on to it. In a week, you pop back in and take out £10. Two weeks later you go back in and take out another £10, by which time someone else has put £100 into a new account. Pretty soon the bank realises that it is sitting on the best part of £180 while waiting for you and the other person to come and ask for it all back. But as this doesn't happen, they realise pretty quickly that they can lend out £90 of your money and earn themselves interest in the meanwhile, because you are not going to ask for more than £10 of your deposit.

So then a clever idea occurs. If that ratio of 9:1 is safe and true, then it is always safe and true. It means that those who hold accounts will never ask for more than ten per cent of their money at any one time. So the bank can be a little more ambitious. If you put in £100 into your account, the bank can lend £900 and still be within that 9:1 ratio. The only difference is that the £900 they lent is not real money. It is backed up by the £100 you put in, but only up to the point where people draw out money *under normal circumstances*. If, on the other hand, circumstances turn abnormal and there is a run on the bank, the bank is not in a position to say, 'just wait while we call in the £100 you deposited because they have to account for the other £900 of 'fictional' money. That is why the whole system rests on stability, and stability rests entirely on confidence.

In fact, over time, this becomes established as a rule, and banks become wedded to this 9:1 ratio. In fact, this is embedded into international banking protocols, called the Basel accords, as well as in national regulation. That means that as long as a bank has ten per cent of its money on reserve it can lend out another ninety per cent to the public – but no more. That is how banks traditionally create money; most have us have borrowed money from a bank, and once it's agreed the loan amount appears in our account. The bank hasn't given us cash to deposit in the bank, it has made a book transfer. That's how it works.

Things go swimmingly, with the banks lending ninety per cent of their holdings – their capital – that we have deposited. After all, they are still dealing with real money. We did put £100 in your account and the bank merely redirected £900 into a loan.

But the lending doesn't stop there. When the £900 that a bank has lent you enters your account, that bank also treats this like a cash deposit and may well lend out ninety per cent (£810) of that; of that £810 deposited in another account the bank may well lend out ninety per cent (£729) of that. That goes on and on until you get almost to zero. So the original £100 that was deposited has created a cascading series of loans. That is how retail banks, not the Bank of England, create ninety-seven per cent of all the money in the economy.[96]

So money can be created out of thin air, but it can also be used repeatedly as it circulates around the system a number of times. This is called the multiplier effect. The combination of actual cash banks have in reserve, the money they create and the number of times they circulate it is close to how the Bank of England and the Treasury calculate how much money there is in the economy or, as they call it, the size of the money supply. This is important, because the amount of money that circulates in the economy has a direct impact on GDP. In the scenario above all the money lent is spent in the high street and that is what we classify as 'consumer spending'. Think back to Chapter Two – as it represents about sixty-five per cent of a calculation of GDP, the circulation of money which supports consumer spending feeds into the GDP.

This means that banks can have a fundamental influence on GDP, as they can artificially pump money into, or suck money out of, the economy. A lot of us, for example, benefitted from the steep increase in house prices in the 2000s by increasing the amount we borrowed through our mortgages using some of the increased value of our homes. This is, again, fictitious value, as the increase in house value is based on the 'market', which is an estimate by estate agents of what someone will pay for your house.

Nevertheless, we borrowed plenty of money using housing equity renewal, so much so that the amounts the banks lent us in this way increased from £4bn in 2001 to peak at almost £18bn in 2004. That means banks pumped between £10 and 14bn per year into the system during the 2000s. We used this to buy cars, holidays and home improvements that fed straight into the consumer spending element of GDP. The UK economy grew by around 2.8 per cent in 2003–4; the amount of extra money pumped into the economy by the banks through housing equity renewal alone was £14bn, or 1.1 per cent of GDP.[97] And this is just one of the ways in which banks pumped money into the economy. You can add to this business loans, credit cards and small loans. In fact, in 2007 our UK banks created £567,000,000,000.[98]

After the credit crunch and the squeeze on the banks, housing equity withdrawal was negative £5–8bn per year. More money was repaid by us than was lent by banks, which sucked around £15bn out of our economy in just one year.[99] Bank lending to businesses fell from a peak of around £150bn in 2007 to a trough of less than £40bn by the end of 2009[100]. They did this by, amongst other measures, cancelling overdrafts, not issuing loans, and cancelling existing loans.

The net effect of this drop in lending was a drop in the amount of the money in the economy. That left less to be spent in shops, leading to shops not doing enough business and having to make people unemployed. That is how less money and less spending and less investment in the economy reduce GDP, creating negative growth, which increase unemployment and increase the deficit.

So banks can pump up and deflate GDP. Visually this would look like gas being pumped in and out of a gas cylinder. Is that where the deficit is?

This works fine so long as the public has confidence in the bank. That way, everyone is happy to leave their money there. If confidence falls, people will rush in to take their money out – there is a 'run' on the banks. That would be disastrous, because the bank would have to recall your money from the people to whom it had been loaned. Some of them will be small companies, and having to repay bank loans could mean closing their business and laying off workers.

This is what happened to the Fidelity Fiduciary Bank. After telling Michael and Jane Banks that England will fall if the banks do, Mr Dawes walks over to them. (Remember they are backed into a corner.) Michael opens his hand to check the tuppence is still in there, and Mr Dawes seizes the opportunity and snatches the money out of his hand. 'Welcome to our joyful family of investors,' he gleefully declares. Michael is appalled, 'Give it back!' he demands, but Mr Dawes refuses. The customers waiting at the bank tellers in the main atrium of the bank can hear the commotion: 'There's something wrong. The bank won't give someone their money!' Bank customers rush to the tellers and demand all the money they have in their accounts. Soon there is a huge queue of people demanding their money back and more running to get into the bank. The Fidelity Fiduciary Bank is in chaos. Officials are running around closing safes, emptying tills and fighting with customers to close the huge bank doors.

The same sort of thing happened to Northern Rock on 15 September 2007. When the public lost confidence, depositors turned up at the branches to get their money out. It was a classic 'run'. The BBC reported, 'banking sources suggest that on Friday alone clients pulled out £1bn – or 4–5% of retail deposits.'[101] The BBC later said that £2bn was withdrawn in cash, running down Northern Rock's reserves, as queues built up outside branches and down streets. In Glasgow, the police were even called to deal with boisterous customers.

So how did this happen? The answer takes us into the heart of the banking crisis. In the 1990s and early 2000s there was a massive increase in mortgage lending in the USA. Selling loans had shifted to more than 7 million people on low incomes and people with poor credit history – people who otherwise would be considered too risky for a normal loan. This was called the 'subprime market'. Although the interest was higher than the interest on normal loans, people were persuaded to buy a house because the introductory repayment offers were so low. US banks lent over $2 trillion in this way.

The Federal National Mortgage Association ('Fannie Mae') and the Federal Home Loan Mortgage Corporation ('Freddie Mac') were established by the US government to increase home ownership by making federal money available for lending to mortgage applicants. By 2007 they were operating like investment wholesalers themselves, buying up mortgages from banks and packaging them into bundles, which they then sold on as investments to other financial institutions. These investments are called mortgage-backed securities, and they were considered stable investments because they were backed by twenty or more years of guaranteed mortgage repayments. That's what the credit agencies thought as well, and gave these securities a AAA rating.

These investments were considered low risk not only because the vast majority of customers could be relied upon to make mortgage repayments, but because the houses the mortgages had been used to purchase were increasing in value. The banks couldn't lose; if the borrower couldn't pay, the banks would keep the house, which would be worth more than they were owed from the loan anyway. But the growth of the subprime market meant that banks were lending to people who had very little hope of paying them back.

So, now we have a bank lending a mortgage to an individual house buyer. This mortgage, together with other mortgages this bank and others lend, are bundled into packages and bought by Freddie Mac and Fannie Mae. As the value of property was increasing, the house as an asset was worth more than the actual mortgage. That made the investment worth more than the original mortgage, which is why Fannie Mae and Freddie Mac had ready buyers for these investments. As Acharya and Richardson explain it, 'a bank pays $100,000 for a mortgage valued at $115,000. The bank profits by selling the mortgage at any price above $100,000, while the investor should end up making a profit by purchasing the mortgage at any price below $115,000. In effect, the bank trades expected future income for income in the present.'[102] But it doesn't end there.

The banks who bought these mortgage-package investments could not be entirely sure that they were all worth what they were told, so they took out insurance. If the investment became worthless, the insurance company would pay the bank the full original value that the bank had paid for the investment. The insurance of an investment is called a 'credit default swap'. AIG, the American insurance company, was one of the biggest insurer of investments. In fact, by 2008, the credit default market was worth $50 trillion, four times the GDP of the USA.

The credit default market operates its own liquidity ratio, one based on the assumption that 'the chance of a lot of debts defaulting at the same time is tiny'.[103] David Malone, author of *Debt Generation*, followed the unfolding banking disaster, and reckoned that AIG could insure $3–4bn of swaps with a cash reserve of just $80 million to cover them (a liquidity ratio of about 1:45). But with 'risky' investments that were backed up by insurance companies, the banks couldn't lose. UK banks loved the idea of buying these securities so much that they spent more money on buying investments than on making personal and business loans. RBS, Barclays, HBOS and others bought up billions of pounds worth of them. They calculated that they could get a higher return on their money through buying investments (government bonds and mortgage-backed securities) than they could from traditional retail banking activity. This is what has become known as 'casino banking' and the money they were using to place their bets was the money banked by depositors – including *us*.

But remember, banks are only allowed to use ninety per cent of the money they hold in deposits. As there was so much money to be made, they found a way around the 9:1 liquidity ratio rule, by creating stand-alone companies that were wholly owned by the bank. They were called Single Purpose Vehicles (SPVs). Although formally independent companies, they were actually an arm of the banks themselves, and this device allowed the banks to buy and sell investments (securities) to get around the constraint of a 9:1 ratio. Lots of the banks set these up, into what became in effect a shadow and unregulated banking system. How did this work?

As an example, a bank that had £10m of cash on deposit could lend only up to £90m in loans because of the 9:1 liquidity ratio. To be able to create more money, the bank sold £40m of the loans to its Single Purpose Vehicle, thus removing £40m from its balance sheet, as if these loans magically no longer existed. As the bank regulators could not audit the SPV, it looked like the bank now had the capacity to lend or spend another £40m. In reality, though, the bank had £10m on deposit, but had now lent £130m. That is a 13:1 ratio; and that was how banks were able to lend money hand over fist in the early 2000s.

The Single Purpose Vehicle did not only buy the securities from the bank, but would then package them up with other loans (securities) and sell them on as investments, just like Fannie and Freddie did. The more it bought and sold, the more of the banks' loans the Single Purpose Vehicle could buy. In this way, despite all the national and international banking regulations to the contrary, RBS ended up owing 35 times what it was worth by 2006. By then virtually the whole of the UK banking system was based on buying and selling assets, underpinned by a property market that was continually growing in value. Banks became cash flow businesses. No wonder Mr Dawes was so keen to get his hands on Michael's tuppence.

This is a classic pyramid scheme with default swaps at the top and mortgage-backed securities underneath, all underpinned by someone's mortgage and someone's house at the bottom.

What happened next? When the introductory mortgage periods ended, the high interest rates for subprime mortgages kicked in. Millions of people in the USA found that they couldn't afford to meet the repayments and started to foreclose on their mortgages. Millions of houses were returned to the bank, and as a result the number of houses now on the market was far greater than the demand; house prices fell. That meant the value of the house the bank had now reclaimed was worth less than the mortgage, and there was no one to sell the houses on to anyway. For example a house in Detroit that was mortgaged at $88,000 in 2001 was on the market in 2008 for $1,250.[104] This happened across huge swathes of US housing estates. As the houses lost value, so did the mortgage-backed securities – indeed, they became virtually worthless. Banks and their Single Purpose Vehicles were sitting on investments that were now worth nothing, and no one wanted to buy them. Banks had lost one of their key sources of money, and were stuck with a huge cash flow problem with a large number of worthless assets.

The banking system was infested with worthless subprime mortgage-backed securities, because they were packaged up and sold with good mortgage investments. We'll let David Malone continue: 'They mixed these tin mortgages into packages with solid gold ones. They then sold the lot on pretending it was all gold.'[105] The banks and financial institutions that had bought billions of dollars worth of what were now worthless mortgage-backed securities then turned to AIG to pay out on the credit default swaps – their investment insurance – but the sheer number of housing defaults and worthless mortgages was so great that AIG did not have the money to pay out their insurance. Remember they insured investments at a value many times more than the cash they actually had. They couldn't pay out. Banks were left penniless, and called on Alistair Darling. The whole pyramid came tumbling down.

But the banks and the Single Purpose Vehicles had to borrow money from somewhere to buy the investments in the first place and keep the circulation of money going: each other. Banks that had the capacity to lend would lend to other banks, most commonly over the very short term, and often overnight. In effect those banks were borrowing the money to make sure they had enough cash to cover its transactions for that day. These short term loans were essential to grease the wheels of bank lending and keep the system functioning. But this is incredibly volatile and shows how close to the edge banks were operating.

But this wasn't just an American folly. We discussed this with an advisor from RBS. The advisor worked in the security department and was a veteran of the bank lending boom in the 2000s. 'I met one customer last week,' he told us, 'who has a property portfolio of £5m and has an annual salary of £22,000.' This was dumbfounding. How can that happen? 'In the early 2000s if a customer wanted a mortgage that was worth seventy-five per cent or less of the value of the property, the credit check machines were switched off.' So the £5m portfolio guy built one mortgage on top of another by borrowing on the equity of one house to pay a twenty-five per cent deposit on his next house – and so on.

The whole project was based on the customer being able to rent out all or most of his properties. But with the credit crunch he was left with some empty houses, which meant the rent he was getting was not enough to cover all his mortgage repayments. And then the value of property had gone down, which meant he couldn't even sell them, because they were worth less than the mortgages he had. It is an allegory of the whole crumbling banking system.

How was this allowed to happen? Over the years, bank arrangements and regulation have degraded as, step by step, the banks have changed their status from traditional retail lenders to speculative investors. That means that the subprime lending was massive in the UK as well, and usually associated with buy-to-let properties. There are about 1.2 million of them, and virtually all this lending started in the 1990s. The Halifax and Nationwide put the average UK house price at around £165,000 which makes the amount of bank money invested in this subprime market approach £195bn. This is where a lot of the banks' invented money went, and since the government relaxed capital gains tax on second homes to the point where it is difficult to pay capital gains tax on selling a second home even if you tried, this money is a private pool of profit for banks, out of the reach of Revenue and Customs. But this is also where negative equity and rental cash flow has created a subprime market in the UK itself. Many of these mortgages were given to people who would not normally be eligible to borrow this amount of money. That is how our friend at RBS ended up with such an improbable housing portfolio.

Much of this reckless banking activity is a product of the last twenty to thirty years. 'The subprime crisis had shown how a problem in one part of the world could infect the entire system within months or even weeks, not years as in the past.'[106] But how was it allowed to happen?

The 1900 Gold Standard Act legislated for a time when the dollar was backed literally by its weight in gold. This was formalised in the Bretton Woods System in 1946, when the dollar became the fixed point for the world system of currency exchange rates. This created a system of fixed exchange rates that allowed governments to sell their gold to the United States Treasury at $35 per ounce. The whole world of currencies was backed by the value of gold. It meant, in effect, that all currencies' values were set in relation to the dollar and the dollar itself was fixed to the price of gold. No wonder Fort Knox became such an emblematic institution.

But in 1971, President Nixon broke the link between the value of gold and the value of currencies, as the USA came off the gold standard. For the first time ever, all currencies were now free floating, with their value dependent on how much people and speculators wanted to buy and sell them for. Currencies became prey to the market and their value was based on what traders and speculators wanted to pay for them.

Up to this point American banks offered mortgages at rates of interest that were higher than the rate at which they were borrowing money. That was until 1982, when Congress passed the Garn-St Germain Depository Institution Act, which allowed American banks to offer mortgages at variable rates of interest, even if they were lower than the bank rate. Banks could now offer low rates of interest as introductory incentives to lenders, something that we now take for granted as a normal feature of bank lending. We in the UK have benefitted from this a lot in the past twenty years, where initial mortgage interest rates were as low as two per cent for two to five years, before increasing to a higher rate for the lifetime of the mortgage. Many of us exploited the market to jump from mortgage to mortgage, instead of paying the higher, proper rate of interest.

At the same time, banking traditionally only sold financial products within their own country, and each area of the world had its own stock exchange. The Nikkei was in Japan, the NASDAQ and the Dow were American, the DAX was German and the FTSE was the London Stock Exchange. If you travelled to New York in 1979, you would only see American banks. You wouldn't see a branch of NatWest or Midland bank – RBS or HSBC today. There were only country-owned banks. In fact, in the USA there were mainly state-based banks.

The development of the internet allowed the linking-up of all the world's leading stock markets. They could list major companies throughout the world, trading twenty-four hours a day through each time zone. This is why on the news, commentators report the stock market in the UK at close of business in the evening and await the reaction of the Japanese and US markets. This helped to create the international flow of money. But it also represented the deregulation of the UK financial market (and the relaxing of liquidity ratios) that led to an influx of American banks and financial speculating institutions into London. This all happened in 1986 through what was called the 'Big Bang', which was 'the start of investment banking in the UK,' says Tony Dolphin, chief economist at the Institute for Public Policy Research.[107] This was a step change in the international flow of money.

So NatWest could start to trade in the USA and Goldman Sachs could trade in Britain, Japan, or anywhere else for that matter. Subprime mortgage investments prepared in the United States could be bought in the UK by RBS. It opened up international dealing on a scale that had not been possible before. Return to New York in 2012, and this time you see branches of HSBC, RBS and Barclays. These are no longer just British banks, but global ones.

Despite such developments, banks continued to make money from traditional retail banking – issuing loans and taking deposits. That was until 1999, when the USA passed the Gramm-Leach-Bliley Act, which allowed banks to combine investment and retail banking. All of a sudden cash deposited in retail banks could be used for the buying and selling of investments, what is now called 'casino banking', and could use their deposits as collateral. That was the last piece of the bank deregulation jigsaw. From 1971, when the USA came off the gold standard, until today, the banks have been able to speculate with currency, offer loans with variable interest, trade internationally and start to speculate with investments using the money we deposit in the bank. Throw into this mix the commitment of Alan Greenspan to the financial sector in 1987, following a stock market crash, 'The Federal Reserve, consistent with its responsibilities as the nation's central bank, affirmed today its readiness to serve as a source of liquidity to support the economic and financial system.'[108] Now you can see how Goldman Sachs, Lehman Brothers, Citicorps and AIG could think they were too big to fail.

Back in the UK our banks were mimicking their American cousins with the exponential growth of RBS. RBS, despite being the smaller entity, bought out NatWest, which was the UK's fifth largest bank in 2000. It then started to buy up banks elsewhere and to speculate in American mortgage-backed securities and government bonds from countries all over the world. As we now know, it ended up building up liabilities thirty-five times what it was worth.

The Thatcher government of the 1980s restructured the UK economy, although it continued a trend that had started in the 1970s, facilitating a shift in dependence from manufacturing to finance. The Big Bang was the deal-breaker, and led to a huge expansion of the financial sector in the City of London and its growing influence on the UK economy. From 1970 to 2010 the financial services sector's contribution to UK GDP rose from four per cent to nine per cent, while at the same time the manufacturing sector saw a decline from thirty per cent to twelve per cent.[109] These were seismic shifts.

The combination of all these regulatory changes allowed banks to change the way they operated, moving further away from localised, traditional retail banks. Prior to deregulation, banks were able to create money that would fuel economic expansion by investing in tangible assets and products. Small and large businesses took advantage of the ninety per cent fictional money to create wealth. But ultimately the money was backed up by something tangible – British cars, farm produce, engineering, shipbuilding. So fictional money made manufacturing output possible, and at the same time manufacturing output collateralised fictional money.

Meanwhile, the banks were the engines of growth, creating money where needed, making a profit, serving the needs of their customers – and respecting and valuing their customers because they were the foundation of the whole system. For their part, customers respected banks and took confidence from the inherent conservatism of the bank, which came from the disciplines of liquidity ratios. The Bank of England imposed the 9:1 ratio as a regulation to keep the financial institutions safe and within the bounds of what could be managed in a crisis.

After the Big Bang, banks made hay. Of course, they had to back up the loans they were making somehow or another. One way of doing this was to get into the property market in a big way. Property was a long-term asset and allowed for long-term debt. If you lent £50,000 to someone to buy a house they would have twenty-five years to pay it off – and the bank could sell the promise of that pay-off for up to twenty-five years, as we saw before with the growth of Single Purpose Vehicles. Property was good business and displaced liquidity ratios which held the banks back into the short-term. Buy-to-let was an especially attractive option for bank property portfolios since it offered a way of selling multiple homes to the same person – effectively using individuals as their agents in profiteering from rented property.

But, as we have seen, the banks moved ever more heavily into investments, usually government bonds and mortgage-backed securities, which sent liquidity ratios into orbit. They had shifted their activity from investing in concrete things – factories, ships, houses – things of real value, into financial investments that were at some distance from real value. These were markets for promises over debts and were often divorced from concrete capital, fuelled by the desire to earn exotic salaries and bonuses and to wield power. They were gambles, bits of paper with only a nominal value that were bought and sold. So, despite the fact that banking activity created a huge increase in the amount of money in the economy, because it did not support business investment it had a limited impact on growth.

The net result of using customer deposits to finance casino banking, and shifting mortgages off the bank's balance sheet onto an SPV, was that the amount of money the banks were lending as a proportion of cash deposits grew. Remember that international agreements pegged this liquidity ratio at 9:1 – but as the banks found a way around this, they ended up lending out thirty-five times what they had in cash deposits.

In 2007–8 Northern Rock was going bust, as were RBS and HBOS. The government was fearful that this would lead to a collapse of the entire banking system in the UK, and resolved to implement what we now know as the 'bank bailout'. Darling and Brown decided that the government needed to provide a range of financial support that would prevent the banks from collapsing.

The support included purchasing bank shares, guaranteeing deposits in UK and Icelandic Banks, providing a cap on any losses from toxic debts and using government money to inject capital into banks by buying back UK government bonds they had bought. The initiatives were all lumped under what was called the Financial Services Compensation Scheme, Special Liquidity Scheme, Asset Purchase Facility Fund and an Asset Protection Scheme. You can probably work out which is which. But the point to make is that the value we as a country placed on these schemes represented what was in effect the value of a banking deficit. The gap between what the banks had as deposits and income, and what they owed – that same equation as in the fiscal deficit.

We valued this support at £1,020bn.[110] In 2008 this was the equivalent of eighty-five per cent of our GDP – higher than the total UK national debt, which was around £800bn at the time. But what was the response to this from the government? Did we need to cut back bank spending? No. Did we ask staff to cut back on their bonuses and salaries? No. In fact the response to the bank deficit was to pump in extra money. Bankers' and government's concerns with fiscal deficit are with the spending side of the equation; but with the bank deficit it is with the income side of the equation. Since 2009, we have pumped an additional £375bn into the banks through Quantitative Easing. This is basically electronic money from the Bank of England, which is buying up government bonds that the banks and pension funds are holding. It is a simple way of pumping money into banks, and at the same time buying up government bonds – or government borrowing. The government is in essence buying its own debt (bonds) back from the banks.

By the way, if you remember how Iceland used bailout money to help its people, there is nothing to stop the Bank of England using this electronic transfer of funds to reduce our mortgage payments or credit card debt, or to give everyone £1,000 as long as it is spent within a month. All of this is an option. Japan did that, Iceland achieved that, but in the UK no one is interested.

By 2010 the exposure of the government to the banks had reduced to £512bn. But what is the timescale for banks to pay off this deficit? Is it in four years? Indeed, is there any other timescale?

Perhaps the National Audit Office can shed some light on this: 'It is likely that a substantial proportion of these schemes and investments will be with us for some time … In the meantime, the government carries an estimated £5 billion a year cost of financing the shares and loans, and may have to invest more in the future to protect the current value of its investments.'[111] So in other words, not even the National Audit Office knows when the banks will repay their deficit/debt. The banks do not have to reduce their deficit by half or by 100 per cent in four years. In fact there is no knowing how long we, as a country will have to finance the banking deficit.

And it is no wonder when you see what the banks have been doing with this money. They have been using it to continue to finance their speculative activity, as they are certainly not lending to businesses and individuals with any great enthusiasm. In fact, at the end of 2010, the New Economics Foundation painted a very gloomy picture of the future of our banks:

> Based on Bank of England data, banks now appear to face a funding cliff. In order to maintain existing levels of activity they currently have to borrow £12 billion a month; the projections we reproduce in this report indicate that in 2011 they will have to borrow £25 billion a month. We believe the public sector is likely, once again, to be asked to bail out the banks for the emerging funding gap.[112]

What is more, the New Economics Foundation was forecasting that the banks will need to borrow almost twice as much as the UK government does. They weren't wrong. In October 2011, the

Bank of England pumped £75bn through Quantitative Easing into the banks, followed by £50bn in July 2012.

Not only is there no deadline for bank bailout loan repayment, but the government is expected to borrow money to invest in the banks, which is costing us £5bn per year in repayments. If you remember, the single narrative argument makes the case that our interest payments are unmanageable, at £43bn per year. Well £5bn of that is the cost of our government borrowing in order to support the banks, and you don't hear many people complain about that. How interesting it is to see the difference between reducing a public and a bank deficit. The public sector deficit requires cuts, whereas the banking deficit requires investment. If we can borrow to invest in the banks, why can't we borrow and invest in the country's economy?

We are also told that the public deficit must be reduced in half or 100 per cent in four years, yet the banks have no timescale for a reduction of their deficit. Why are these different? What is so special about banks? As if we had to ask.

VI
Politics, Not Economics

An economist is an expert who will know tomorrow why
the things he predicted yesterday didn't happen today.
– Dr Laurence J Peter

Shares in American super-bank Citicorps fell from a high of
$57 a share on December 2006 to ninety-seven cents by May
2009.[113] That wiped over £250bn from the value of one of the
United States' biggest banks. Deutsche Bank shares fell from
a high of €86.64 in June 2007 to €18.22 in December 2009.
And who predicted that?

These banks have highly qualified and highly paid economists
working for them. And this is what they are supposed to do:

An economist is a vital part of the operations of financial
institutions, global asset management organisations and
charitable foundations. Professional incumbents are prized
for their acumen in areas that include currency movements,
financial analyses and shifts of political power.[114]

This is what employment specialists tell us, in case we would
like to apply.

Most large companies employ analysts like this. But who
of these experienced, expert economists in Deutsche Bank or
Citicorps predicted that share prices and the very solvency of
these banks were at stake prior to the credit crunch? Not many.

Iceland's was the first of the insolvent bank ducks to fall when
the credit crunch drifted over from the United States in 2006–7.
The country had three banks that offered interest rates that were
so good that lots of UK local authorities and charities switched

large deposits to them. The Icelandic banks ended up with a turnover/liability, which was 1,400 per cent of Iceland's total GDP. This is a country with a population of less than 350,000 and a government that boasted of being debt free. So their financial activity was a bit like Doncaster Rovers playing in the Champions League, or a corner post office branch bidding to buy RBS. But because the Icelandic banks' borrowing was financed by international banks, they and the country needed annual independent assessments of their financial status and risk to make sure that everything was hunky dory.

In 2006, Tryggvi Herbertsson, an economist at the University of Iceland, and Frederic Mishkin, a Columbia Economics professor who later was to become a governor of the Federal Reserve in the USA, penned their 'Financial Stability in Iceland' report. Was there any doubt in their minds that such small banks in such a small country were able to carry the huge amount of debt they had? Well Mishkin and Herbertsson told us that, 'although Iceland's economy does have imbalances that will eventually be reversed, financial fragility is not high and the likelihood of a financial meltdown is very low.'[115] Iceland went bust on an unprecedented scale less than eighteen months later.

In September 2006 American economist Nouriel Roubini addressed an International Monetary Fund conference of the world's most senior economists. He was reflecting on the state of the international financial system, and told his audience of his forecast that homeowners would soon start to default on mortgages, meaning trillions of dollars of mortgage-backed securities would become worthless and the global financial system would collapse. He predicted that hedge funds, investment banks and other major financial institutions would collapse, and he even named Fannie Mae and Freddie Mac. He could not have been more accurate. And what was the response to that? The moderator of the event quipped, 'I think perhaps we will need a stiff drink after that.' People laughed.[116] Roubini was written off as a 'perpetual pessimist' and a 'career naysayer'. He was proven correct twelve months later.

So virtually all of the world's most experienced and qualified economists in the biggest banks in the world, and working in the world's greatest financial institutions, missed the biggest economic cardiac arrest in their lifetime. They missed the biggest recession and financial breakdown since the 1930s, if not ever. Have any of them apologised or made their excuses? Has there been a rethink of the state and condition of economics as a discipline? No. Are they still advising countries and corporations? Yes.

And what are they telling us now? Well, a majority of them are telling us that public sector cuts will work fine in bringing the UK out of debt and recession. Forty-three of the seventy-eight economists questioned by the *Financial Times* in 2010 thought the deficit reduction plan of the UK government would put our finances and our economy on track, 'most concluded that the austerity measures, including today's rise in the rate of value added tax to twenty per cent, were a big gamble, but one that was likely to pay off.'[117] That means that the same economists who missed the credit crunch are now telling us that public sector cuts will work.

Not only that, but after putting their authority behind what have since been seen to be dodgy UK economic forecasts, what has actually happened? The UK government forecasts for growth and borrowing in 2010 have not just been a little out, they have been way, way out. The actual growth has turned out to be zero, against a forecast of 2.8 per cent. The Chancellor forecast that the UK would borrow £471bn over six years in 2010, but this has already been revised up to £650bn over seven years, and that is without the borrowing for 2012–13 now predicted to be

£30bn higher than even the revised forecasts. That is over fifty per cent wrong.

Yet these same economists are also invited by BBC and ITV editors to come onto their news programmes to provide 'independent' comment on the latest GDP figures or other economic news. How do we know who these people are and how independent they are when they appear on our screens, radios or in our newspapers? Take Frederic Mishkin, professor of Economics at Columbia University. He was paid $134,858 by Iceland's banks to produce an *'independent'* report that confirmed that the banks were in a good position, and was a governor of the Federal Reserve Bank at the time. So who is he representing when he makes his economic assessment? We already noted that the USA Federal Treasury Secretary that 'hammered' through a bank bailout that benefited Goldman Sachs was Goldman Sachs' former CEO, Hank Paulson.

So when corporate economists are asked to comment by the BBC on the eurozone or the state of the UK economy, are they bringing their expertise to bear to comment on employment, housing, health, the country's benefit? No, because they have to use their skills to the benefit of the business they are working in, not the country they live in. They must be 'capable of influencing senior management to use this analysis to shape decisions throughout the business.' The likes of Barclays Bank has £40bn of Greek, Spanish and Portuguese debt, RBS has lent £50bn to Ireland, French banks have over £300bn exposure to Italy and Spain, and German banks have lent £101bn alone to Italy. So how can Deutsche Bank, Santander, Bank Paribas or JP Morgan economists comment independently on the eurozone crisis, when they are working for the banks owed money by the very countries that they are being asked to comment on?

We've heard how the economists at the IMF laughed at Nouriel Roubini's prediction of financial collapse, yet twelve months later he was proven right. And we've heard that their catastrophic error of judgement hasn't stopped these same economists making authoritative judgements since on the UK economy. In September 2010 they told us with absolute assurance and authority that the unprecedented austerity package the country had embarked on, was right. Their official statement said that 'the UK economy is on the mend. Economic recovery is underway, unemployment has stabilized, and financial sector health has improved'.[118] Before any of these economists make a comment, would it not be reasonable to ask them what their view of the world economy was in 2006?

Then, in June 2011, when the government's economic forecast on growth had been revised down and borrowing revised up, did the IMF think that there needed to be a change in government policy? 'According to IMF staff analysis the answer is no.'[119] John Lipksy, the acting head of the IMF at the time, told us. But why was it not time to change economic policy, John? 'We expect that the deviations from the economic trajectory that had been forecast, to be largely temporary... looking ahead we expect the economic recovery to resume in 2011.' But it didn't, did it? Once the UK had moved into recession in 2012 and borrowing costs were increasing, in direct contradiction to what the government and the IMF had predicted, we were told what we already knew: 'Recovery has stalled. Post-crisis repair and rebalancing of the UK economy is likely to be more prolonged than initially envisaged. Confidence is weak and uncertainty is high.'[120] Couldn't they have seen this coming?

Did the IMF refer to its reports of the previous two years that were completely wrong? Not really. Instead, with the same authority that it told us that the UK government's economic plan was absolutely right, it is now telling us it is not right at all: 'If growth does not take off and unemployment fails to recede even after substantial further monetary stimulus and strong credit easing measures have been given time to work, the policy response should include a further slowing of fiscal consolidation.' In other words, ease up on the cuts and pump some money into the economy. Why didn't the IMF economists tell us that two years ago?

To answer that question, we need to look at what the IMF was set up to do and what it has done since. It was originally established to 'foster global monetary cooperation, secure financial stability, facilitate international trade, promote high employment and sustainable economic growth, and reduce poverty around the world.'[121] John Maynard Keynes was an architect of the IMF, as a response to a post-war world that required international co-operation and country rebuilding on a massive scale. Its aims reflect the post-war aspirations of a 'good' world that would emerge from the trauma and destruction of a war that had engulfed most of the world for six years. It was like a built-in international stabilizer that would create greater equality between nations or at least a safety net to prevent countries with weaker economies from descending into financial chaos and social strife.

Economic stability would help sustain peace. Cordell Hull, the United States Secretary of State, told the Bretton Woods Conference in 1944 that set up the IMF that '[U]nhampered trade dovetailed with peace; high tariffs, trade barriers, and unfair economic competition, with war… if we could get a freer flow of trade… freer in the sense of fewer discriminations and obstructions… so that one country would not be deadly jealous of another and the living standards of all countries might rise, thereby eliminating the economic dissatisfaction that breeds war, we might have a reasonable chance of lasting peace.'[122] Noble aims, and it all started so well, providing support for reconstruction in Europe, with few strings attached.

But by the 1970s this had all changed. A new breed of economists had taken over, one that demanded more intrusive changes to a country's economy in return for an IMF loan. In Chile from 1975 to 1983, the IMF supported one of the world's nastiest dictators, General Augusto Pinochet, with over £300m of loans, but only in exchange for a change in economic policy, which included, 'three strategic thrusts: completely integrating Chile into the capitalist world market by destroying protectionism and debauching the currency; fighting inflation by drastically reducing government expenditures and government employment; and eliminating practically all nationalist checks on the entry and operations of foreign capital'.[123] Now that sounds familiar doesn't it? The IMF insisted on privatising public assets and reducing public services, pay and pensions.

Argentina had economic problems of its own, prompting help and loans from the IMF throughout the 1990s, culminating in 2001 with economic and social disaster. Any strings attached to IMF support? 'Although the IMF pumped in additional funds, it provided these funds on the condition that the Argentine government would entirely eliminate its budget deficit.'[124] How did the IMF propose to do that? 'With the economy in a nose-dive and tax revenues plummeting, the only way to balance the budget was to drastically cut government spending.' Where have we seen that solution to economic problems since? In Greece, where the government is being forced to reduce public spending and sell off public assets, so that foreign banks from the key member states of the IMF are repaid. And Ireland. And Portugal. And Spain...

Greece is now in the midst of a major social crisis. Unemployment has risen to over twenty-two per cent, twenty-seven per cent of people are now living in poverty, as wages, including the minimum wage, have been reduced to a level at which people cannot afford to live. Queues for food parcels amongst the middle classes have grown alarmingly and there are riots on the streets. The country is collapsing.

But before the IMF supported Chile, GDP growth was steady and unemployment was three per cent. Thanks to the support of the IMF, GDP fell by thirteen per cent, unemployment rose by twenty per cent and didn't fall below ten per cent for the whole period of IMF support and industrial production fell by an astounding twenty-seven per cent. Pinochet kept a lid on the social unrest, driven by such inequality, through bloody military repression. Post-IMF intervention in Argentina, unemployment shot up to twenty per cent and there was a massive run on the banks. The years of austerity budgets, pay cuts and public service shrinkage, pushed people to their limit. Serious social unrest broke out across the country, until a state of emergency was finally declared in 2001.

The same story can be told about much of IMF support in sub-Saharan Africa, Mexico and several other countries in Latin America, Thailand and other parts of East Asia hit by the 1997 crisis, in Turkey and now in Greece. A catalogue of increasing national debt, high unemployment, inequality and social unrest. The IMF now has a clear pattern of providing loans, but under condition that the public sector is shrunk, and public pay and pensions are cut.

Britain itself was a victim of the IMF back in November 1976 when, under Chancellor of the Exchequer Denis Healey, it was thought that we had an unsustainable deficit. Healey negotiated a £2.9bn loan in exchange for an austerity programme of £1bn per year (£6bn in today's prices) and set the long-term scene for the collapse of the government under civil unrest (the 'Winter of Discontent'). In numerous interviews in recent years Healey has admitted that this was a mistake and unnecessary. Recently published cabinet minutes show the titanic battle between Healey and other cabinet ministers at the time, who for their part insisted that the alternative to austerity was an industrial growth plan. No wonder the IMF loved UK economic policy in

2010 and 2011: it finished the job they had started thirty-five years previously.

Keynes and his contemporaries argued for the creation of an international financial instrument that would stabilise economies, using economic analysis based on social justice. And it is not fair to say that today there are not economists making similar proposals, or proposals that come from the same school of thought. We have seen that Nobel prize-winners Paul Krugman, Christopher Pissarides, Joseph Stiglitz (former Director of the World Bank), Robert Skidelsky and Professor David Blanchflower (former member of the Bank of England Monetary Policy Committee) still see their economics through the prism of social justice, just as Keynes did. So don't think this is an attack on all economists. We merely point out that there are broadly two traditions: the first was in ascendancy until the 1970s, the other has been since.

Keynes, and others since him, have been drawn on a brand of economics that is driven by a philosophy that is concerned with how to create a more just society, a society in which the way governments and people relate to one another is based on principles of morality. Keynes was an economist of recessions. He witnessed them – including the Great Depression of the 1930s – and he was repulsed by the waste and inefficiency of them. He observed how markets and market forces failed, and the government had to step in to invest in their country to keep the economy going, and keep people in work. Keynes saw governments and national banks as the main tool to break recessions and depressions, because they could pump more than enough money into the economy to get the money and economic activity flowing again. He understood economic 'cycles' – high flow, low flow, 'boom', 'bust', much like the dynamics of the tides – and saw government as the mechanism for engineering more stability to even out the cycle – much as Gordon

Brown achieved for more than ten years as Chancellor. In fact, Keynes was able to apply his approach to international economics and global economic cycles. Remember, he was one of the architects of the International Monetary Fund. His brand of economics influenced or was used by governments in the UK and the USA both pre- and post-war. He also established the basis of a progressive tax system.

In the 1940s and through the 1960s, economics based on social justice was the political consensus. Remember Roosevelt's New Deal in the USA:

We find our population suffering from old inequalities, little changed by vast sporadic remedies. In spite of our efforts and in spite of our talk, we have not weeded out the overprivileged and we have not effectively lifted up the underprivileged. Both of these manifestations of injustice have retarded happiness. No wise man has any intention of destroying what is known as the profit motive; because by the profit motive we mean the right by work to earn a decent livelihood for ourselves and for our families.

We have, however, a clear mandate from the people, that Americans must forswear that conception of the acquisition of wealth which, through excessive profits, creates undue private power over private affairs and, to our misfortune, over public affairs as well. In building toward this end we do not destroy ambition, nor do we seek to divide our wealth into equal shares on stated occasions. We continue to recognize the greater ability of some to earn more than others. But we do assert that the ambition of the individual to obtain for him and his a proper security, a reasonable leisure, and a decent living throughout life, is an ambition to be preferred to the appetite for great wealth and great power.[125]

Harold Macmillan, who was arguably the most influential Conservative Party politician of the time, and was Prime Minister from 1957 to 1963, was of the same ilk. He, like Keynes and Roosevelt, witnessed mass unemployment, 'lessons which I have never forgotten. If, in some respects, they may have left too deep an impression on my mind, the gain was greater than the loss.'[126] That thought must have stayed with him throughout his political life: 'When I am told... that inflation can be cured or arrested only by returning to substantial or even massive unemployment, I reject that utterly.' As Prime Minister he was adamant that government had to play a key role in keeping people in work and avoiding the kind of poverty that had so distressed him. He had also seen what happened if private businesses spectacularly failed, and knew that they needed reining in. 'By the time they left office in 1964, Conservative economic policy had been transformed. In place of the crude attempt to control the economy through the structure of interest rates, there was a whole complex of economic regulators.'[127]

The father of economics is considered to be Adam Smith; his The Wealth of Nations was one of the first economics books, and it analysed the development of capitalism. He wasn't actually an economist, but a Professor of Moral Philosophy, and his work was all dedicated to the design of a fair and just society in which all goods were equally distributed. Inequality, for him, was immoral. This is interesting, because he is considered to be the father of free market economics. The Adam Smith Institute took his name and his theory to develop policy that has supported Thatcherism since the 1970s. The website is unequivocal in its interpretation of Adam Smith, arguing that 'in its early days, the institute was known for its pioneering work on privatization, deregulation, and tax reform, and for its advocacy of internal markets in healthcare and education'.[128] It hasn't changed much since then. But that's not what Smith advocated; he actually thought that the wealthy should be taxed more according to their income: 'The rich should contribute to the public expense, not only in proportion to their revenue, but something more than in that proportion.'[129] Indeed, he saw taxation as an expression of 'liberty', in the sense that contributing to the common good 'liberated' us from a crude and brutal society. He was providing evidence that we can engineer a more just society.

You can see how this gave economics a social context which continued into the modern age. John Maynard Keynes was the most prominent socially-driven economist of them all. He reinvented economics for the large and dynamic economies. He saw society as economically more integrated, a complex machine in which both poor and rich played their part in producing growth. He understood that the lifeblood of an economy was the circulation of money and he focused on how to manage it, how to regulate the circulation so that it was effective, stable and constantly multiplying. In this, he departed from Adam Smith in the most fundamental way. Adam Smith believed in the 'invisible hand'. This was a benevolent market force that would move money around the economy from the rich to the poor without interference. Markets on their own were inherently stable, whereas Keynes replaced the invisible hand with the government as the key tool for the redistribution of income and wealth. This theory held sway after the war until the 1970s.

Since then things haven't half changed. Around the time of the 1960s, predominant economic thought moved away from the inter-war ascendancy of Keynesian economics to a position where it was felt that the hand of government was actually detrimental. Younger economists wanted a free market, or one as free as possible. That's why the IMF in the 1970s began asking for governments to sell off their public assets, as a quid pro quo for giving them money. That's what the experiences of the countries mentioned above of the IMF have in common. Most of this was driven by the United States, not surprisingly, and not least because it was the biggest donor to the IMF and the biggest economy in the world.

The University of Chicago became the home of this school of thought – the home of what was named 'Monetarism'. It produced economists, the leader of whom was Milton Friedman, who ended up being the driving force for US and UK economic policy for the last forty years. They claimed to make economics an objective science, free of the constraints of political and social decisions – for example, Friedman argued that 'the doctrine of 'social responsibility' involves the acceptance of the socialist view that political mechanisms, not market mechanisms, are the appropriate way to determine the allocation of scarce resources to alternative uses'.[130] They analysed countries according to their inflation, GDP and trade deficits – much in the way that a doctor might be said to treat a collection of organs rather than a person. They treated these terms like matters of fact, not matters of value. Remember, GDP is calculated from a survey of around 46,000 businesses and inflation is a survey of 100,000 prices of goods and services from a wide range of retailers. Do they not have more in common with imperfect survey results than with scientific, empirical facts?

Where does this alternative strand of economics come from? For it is an alternative, and it is underpinned by a different moral philosophy. Philosophers like Joseph Schumpeter, writing in the 1930s, asked us to look at the economy as if it were an organism, with needs, demands, stresses and strains, ups and downs. Schumpeter thought that economic booms and busts were as natural to the economy as the changing seasons of the year. As people and organisms grow, Schumpeter told us, so do economies. He described slumps and recessions as if they were like colds and illnesses – natural phenomena. We could no more expect to go through life without illness than an economy can exist without booms and busts. 'Crises' were not disconnected events, Schumpeter went on, but merely elements in a more deep-seated wave-like movement.[131] In Schumpeter's own words, 'the crises are nothing but turning points from prosperity into depression, and it is the alternation between prosperity and depression which is the really interesting phenomenon.'[132] We might catch a cold or flu, but that doesn't stop us growing.

Although Schumpeter was around at the same time as Keynes he drew from a different pool of morality. His economic viewpoint was not based on promoting equality, but on promoting fairness. Have you noticed how this subtle change has come into economic and political language in the last twenty years? Poverty is now 'disadvantage' or 'social exclusion', unemployment is 'worklessness', equality has become 'fairness'. So what's the difference? Fairness is having shops with all the goods in that you would want – equality means that everyone can buy them. Fairness is universities that offer a full range of courses, equality is that we can all access them. Fairness is about creating opportunities, equality is about outcomes. David Cameron thinks 'fairness means giving people what they deserve and what people deserve depends on how they behave'.[133] Equality is not based on what people deserve, but on what they require to be equal. Do you get free NHS care dependent on whether you behaved well in the past twelve months? Do you get a state pension because you behaved well in work? No. You get it because it is what people need to live decent lives.

Policy based on equality creates a progressive tax system, a higher rate of tax for people who earn more, and rebalance for people on lower incomes with lower taxation and more state benefits. Without being dewy-eyed, that's the system we had after the war up to the late 1970s. That is what Norway and Sweden have now, which is why they have a much smaller gap between the higher and lower income earners and why these are much more equal societies, where people enjoy a higher standard of living than the UK. Is that not why in virtually every indicator of the health, education, well-being and happiness of young people both countries score higher than the UK and the USA?[134] Post-war was also a period in our history where gas, electricity and water supply, coal mines, steelworks, the railway system, the car industry, the national airline and airports were government-owned. They may not have operated at peak efficiency, but nationalisation did allow the opportunity to fix prices to reflect the cost of living and social need.

Fairness, on the other hand, is about giving people the opportunity to have a better way of life, but not necessarily helping them to take advantage of it. Does the 'fairness' agenda judge its impact based on well-being or equality? Well, David Cameron asks us to: 'Measure our success by the chance we give.' Perhaps he thinks that if people don't seize the opportunity that's not the government's fault. It would probably have to do with how people behaved. To answer our own question, fairness does not measure outcomes but opportunities. But it is not enough to create opportunities in education, employment and housing if you do not give people the means to take advantage of them. Here's another way of putting it: 'The greatest good to the greatest number of people… is the measure of right and wrong.' Jeremy Bentham said that. He went on to say that in this world and in our way of thinking, actions should be calculated 'on the basis of what is good for the world and not what maximizes the happiness of a particular locality or class'.[135]

In other words as long as most people are okay, economic policies are ok. Or is it okay for people to get more wealthy, as long as people do not become poorer? Policy based on fairness creates a society with lower taxation for the wealthiest in society, less regulation and less state 'interference' in redistribution of income and public services. Policy based on fairness can tolerate an increasing gap between the rich and the poor. That is why Peter Mandelson told an American industrialist in 1998, one year into the New Labour government, that he was 'intensely relaxed about people getting filthy rich as long as they pay their taxes'. [136]

This same mode of thought was exhibited in the 1930s by Schumpeter, who wanted to liberate the entrepreneur and put more cash at his disposal. The key mechanism for driving an economy was not government at all: it was the financial institution – the source of loans and credit. Indeed, he went further: Schumpeter saw capitalism as a headlong rush into growth – occasional crashes – further headlong rushes, with capitalism always reinventing itself through the creativity of the entrepreneur. No wonder Richard Lambert, former director of the Confederation of British Industry, thinks that the government should relax labour laws, reduce corporation tax and remove regulation, because 'private sector investment and trade are the two main engines for growth'. [137]

Schumpeter also gave us the concept of 'creative destruction', where economic busts provide the creative energy for booms and advancement. Recessions, companies closing and rising unemployment are natural phenomena. Bad firms have to close, so that new ones can emerge. Economies have to crash, so that they can readjust and rise again. Unemployment is a side effect, unpleasant depending on your political point of view, but inevitable.

In other words, he is asking us to believe that there is nothing you can do about crashes. In fact, slumps and recessions are good for an economy, 'because they allow for a kind of natural selection: only the sound firms and banks will survive the crisis'. [138] Like a kind of economic Darwinism – survival of the fittest. For people like Schumpeter, 'depressions are nothing but adaptations of the economic system'. [139] So is that why the government can accept increasing unemployment, because it is a natural side effect of a bust? As if our government is powerless to act or would only make things worse if it did. Never mind that the current austerity and cuts mean that people lose their jobs, go hungry, the young have their aspirations dashed and illness and social unrest rise. Watch how Angela Merkel, David Cameron and François Hollande insist that Greece has to make public sector cuts no matter what. In the UK, reducing unemployment is not an economic objective of the Coalition government.

Schumpeter actually saw this system as leading eventually to the destruction of capitalism itself – that, in the end, it is the whole economic system that self-destructs, but creatively. Is this what we are witnessing now? Just how much power do we invest in these free-marketeers? Just how worried do we need to be about their abject and continuing failure to interpret events? It is worth mentioning at this point that the Asian 'tiger' economies have no truck with free markets – they subscribe to a totally different kind of economics. Taiwan, South Korea and Singapore for example, have highly interventionist governments, managed economies, massive government subsidies to industry – and their growth rate never falls below eight per cent per annum. We are falling behind.

The 1970s was fertile ground for this brand of utilitarian economics to grow. It was billed as a science. The Chicago School still tries to kid us that the unifying thread of their economics 'is not political or ideological but methodological, the methodological conviction that economics is an incomparably powerful tool for understanding society'.[140] These economists have been trying to make us believe that they have broken off the shackles of moral philosophy to forge a science that makes objective judgments. For moral philosophy read: political point of view. When you listen to Stephanie Flanders, Evan Davis and Andrew Marr it seems like they treat economic forecasts, judgments and errors as if they have no roots in a moral philosophy or political viewpoint either.

Thatcher and Reagan loved this stuff, and took this brand of free market economics into the heart of their policy. But do you think that they were attracted to this brand of economics because it was a science? Not likely. It suited Margaret Thatcher's moral philosophy – her own sense of social justice: 'What's irritated me about the whole direction of politics in the last 30 years is that it's always been towards the collectivist society.' By collectivist, she meant one with a leading role for government. She and Ronald Reagan wanted to reduce the role of the state in providing an equal society, providing welfare, decent hospitals:

> People have forgotten about the personal society. And they say: do I count, do I matter? To which the short answer is, yes. And therefore, it isn't that I set out on economic policies; it's that I set out really to change the approach, and changing the economics is the means of changing that approach. If you change the approach you really are after the heart and soul of the nation. Economics are the method; the object is to change the heart and soul.[141]

'Free market economics' is not a science – it is an ideology. Isn't that why governments since the 1970s have been relaxed about high unemployment? In the 1980s was that something that Mrs Thatcher thought we would have to live with? 'I think in the short term, yes. In the longer run it will depend on the use people make of the opportunities.'[142] How ambivalent can you be? The policies of austerity of the debt narrative have also created high unemployment, and reducing it has not been the priority or the main economic objective of any political party. The priority has been the reduction of the deficit.

Ironically Thatcher went on to use the very visible hand of government to reduce the public sector and deregulate the private sector to allow the 'market' to function freely. In effect they were taking away all obstacles to people pursuing their own interests and becoming personally wealthy, starting with the 'Big Bang', which we learned in a previous chapter was the touchstone of deregulation. It was the spontaneous relaxation of controls on financial transactions based on the buying and selling of money. Both Reagan and Thatcher believed that the richer some individuals became, the better off everyone would be. No wonder that in this same period, as we have seen in earlier chapters, societies in the UK and the USA became more unequal, tax shifted from direct to indirect, and regulation for banks and private enterprise was relaxed.

This, then, is the shift in the 1970s away from economics based on equality to economics based on encouraging the growth of personal wealth. In the last chapters we have seen what that has done to our societies. Remember the UN Report on Human Development and the Gini Co-efficient, which tell us that the rich are paying less tax now than they were thirty years ago, and that our society has become more unequal year on year in that period? Look at the shift from progressive direct taxation on what you earn to regressive taxation based on what you buy. We have lost control of introducing social cost to the price of electricity, gas, water, rail fares and plane fares, because these once government-owned industries are now entirely private. When Peter Mandelson, architect of New Labour, was telling us he was 'intensely relaxed with people getting filthy rich', Tony Blair told us that his mission would be complete 'when the Labour Party learned to love Mandelson'.[143]

So this change in economic policy was not driven by 'science', but by politics. Moral philosophy still sits behind this government policy, as much as it did the policy of the 1945 Labour government, only the philosophy has changed. Modern economics is just as much about 'the heart and soul'. Remember, David Cameron put morality and 'fairness' at the heart of his deficit reduction policy. Will Hutton observed that 'debt is an issue on which David Cameron and the Conservatives feel they can take the high ground. We cannot go on like this, they insist. The deficit must be cut as a matter of moral urgency.'[144]

'Practical men,' Keynes told us, and we can argue that that includes politicians, 'who believe themselves to be quite exempt from any intellectual influences, are usually slaves of some defunct economist.'[145] But you could also ask by which philosophy is the defunct economist influenced? We never hear of a Chief Economist recommending bailing out the public sector, but hear them frequently arguing to bail out the banks; we always hear them arguing for cutting and never investing more in public services. Deficit reduction at the expense of the public good, as we can now see, is also an ideology. Franklin D Roosevelt put it better than we can: 'While they prate of economic laws, men and women are starving. We must lay hold of the fact that economic laws are not made by nature. They are made by human beings.'[146]

Too many economists today set targets for reducing deficits rather than reducing inequality and poverty, and these too easily elbow out of the media those others who are more anxious about equality. They are closet ideologists. They prefer to produce monthly figures on the level of inflation rather than on levels of health and well-being. Journalists and commentators allow these ideologists to give supposedly 'independent' views without reference to human suffering, or ask why we want to achieve growth. Is that what we have come to? A shrug and resigned acceptance that there is nothing we can do about austerity, the financial squeeze families are experiencing, unemployment, food banks, reduced salaries? Is that what happens when economics in universities is taught as a 'social science' rather than as moral philosophy?

But there is another way. Will Hutton counters Cameron's moral posture on debt: 'Debt morality should never be confused with good economics. Good economics attempts to deliver a functioning economic system that works for all its members.' All, not most of them, you note. 'Necessarily, credit and debt play crucial economic functions, allowing the system to manage the inevitable mismatches between flows of revenue and costs over time. Changes in public debt are a vital instrument to manage the economy efficiently and, crucially, morally and fairly.'[147]

So economics and morality cannot be separated. Economics is not a neutral science – like all sciences, it is a point of view attached to a method. Hutton's position would be even stronger if he extended his point to show that we need to fight austerity, not on economic grounds, but on the grounds of morality itself – on the grounds that it victimizes the vulnerable and actively favours the rich. We should not at all separate these things. Rather, we should do battle over what matters. We should challenge these chief economists, not because we disagree with their economic analysis, but because they represent a repugnant and brutal moral system that is self-serving and ruthless in its punitive logic.

Economics as a discipline is in need of reform, not because it is immoral, but because it is discussed in such a technical, scientific way that we cannot enter into the heart of arguments, for example about austerity and debt. Is it right for a senior executive at BBC news to dismiss a whole strand of political and economic thought from Keynes to Skidelsky because 'it is not realistic to expect us to explore every single academic strand of thinking'? And that when we challenged Evan Davies to give proper air time to anti-austerity arguments he replied saying that this would only 'confuse our audience'? The layperson is precisely the person best equipped to argue economics, because it is about morality and humanism, and it speaks of society as we want it to be. This is a democratic deficit. And that deficit is exactly how an economist was appointed, not elected, as prime minister in Italy and, for a short time, in Greece.

Has economics lost touch with people? Is that not why economists from the IMF can impose policies on the Greek government that trigger untold human misery, impoverishing its people, creating hunger and mass distress? Is that not why the huge bailouts in the UK and the USA did not reduce individual private debt or secure people in their homes by reducing their mortgages? Ed Miliband was right to say that if the 1945 government's only economic objective was to reduce its deficit that it would not have built the welfare state, social housing and the national health service. Why is reducing unemployment not our main economic objective in the UK, rather than reducing the deficit? Why is improving health and well-being, or reducing inequality not our main economic objective? Why is it more important to secure a bank than to secure someone in their home?

Robert Kennedy, on the presidential stump in 1968 six weeks before his assassination, reminded us, that 'the gross national product does not allow for the health of our children, the quality of their education or the joy of their play. It does not include the beauty of our poetry or the strength of our marriages, the intelligence of our public debate or the integrity of our public officials. It measures neither our wit nor our courage, neither our wisdom nor our learning, neither our compassion nor our devotion to our country, it measures everything in short, except that which makes life worthwhile.'[148]

What he was telling us is that economics is a means to an end. It is a tool of government on behalf of society. Like Margaret Thatcher and Ronald Reagan, we need to work out what kind of society we want and use economic tools to help us achieve it – and we can have a more humanistic, compassionate, socially responsible and democratic end in mind than they allowed us. Do we want free healthcare at the point of use, welfare benefits for people unfortunate enough to have to depend on them, pensions for the elderly to live with the comfort of financial security and accessible education for our children and young people? If so then we need to fix our economic policy, taxation, spending, investment and borrowing to achieve our vision. Economics should not drive society, but rather society should drive economics.

VII
Not the Debt Narrative

A people are as healthy and confident as the stories they
tell themselves. Sick storytellers can make nations sick.
Without stories we would go mad. Life would lose its
moorings or orientation.... Stories can conquer fear,
you know. They can make the heart larger.
– Ben Okri

'In conclusion, it is challenging for BBC News to report and
explain complex economic events in a way that engages our
audiences and it is not realistic to expect us to explore every
single academic strand of thinking. Impartiality is not synonymous with blanket comprehensiveness.'

This was the response of a senior BBC executive to our email.
She was replying to a complaint we made to the BBC about the
coverage of the cuts. The final straw for us was the BBC coverage
of the Comprehensive Spending Review in October 2010. Everyone knew that it was going to be a five-year plan of severe,
historically unprecedented cuts to public services, and the BBC
trailed it with six weeks of programmes that included asking us,
the public, to phone in with our suggestions of where these cuts
should fall. They were responding helpfully to George Osborne's
grotesque call for a 'national debate' on whether the weight of
cuts should fall on the public sector or benefit payments – asking
turkeys to choose between Waitrose or Sainsbury's.

How extraordinary. Were NHS nurses expected to pick up
the phone to suggest that they sacrifice their jobs? Or were
people who were unfortunate enough to have to live on welfare
benefits to call to offer to stop claiming? Or maybe the BBC was
waiting for a call from BUPA to suggest that the nearest NHS

hospital be cut? Some of us remember the 1980s, the previous period of significant cuts to the public sector. Only then, they were contentious. The political parties were acrimoniously divided over whether there should have been cuts at all. There were strikes, protests, Thatcher said 'the lady's not for turning', the country was split and unhappy. But there were no BBC programmes that invited us, the public, to make suggestions as to where those cuts should fall. Is this about a crisis of economics – or a crisis of democracy?

Make no mistake, a programme of cuts is a legitimate political ambition, but so is the alternative economic programme. So where was that alternative economic programme represented in 2010? Not on *The Andrew Marr Show*, that's for sure. He interviewed George Osborne days before he announced his Comprehensive Spending or, should we say, the Comprehensive Cuts Review. He is one of our most respected journalists and was the BBC's most senior political journalist, before he was offered his own Sunday morning show. Surely he could be relied on to articulate his skill and forensic questioning to put some pressure on the Chancellor to explain the extent and rationale of the austerity he was proposing? As he sat opposite him, he would more than likely look him square in the eye and challenge his view that the level of cuts we were embarking on were beyond question. No doubt he would throw in a couple of facts about previous levels of debt or examples of failed and successful policies that countries adopted to get themselves out of recession. Did he? Well, we saw earlier what he did say: 'You clearly need to make the savings, the cuts and raise taxes.' Having read this book, can you believe he said that? If he played volleyball that would be have been a great set-up for a spike. Osborne, if you recall, gratefully collected the ball: 'We were on the brink of bankruptcy…' and Marr left that unchallenged as well. We wrote to ask him why. He didn't reply.

He wasn't the only one who did this. John Humphrys was introducing his interview with the Deputy Prime Minister on the Radio 4 *Today* programme the same week. Outside of an interview with Jeremy Paxman, a *Today* interview is known to be amongst the toughest of political arenas. This was also pre-Comprehensive Spending Review and how did John Humphrys open up a challenging interview about the prospect of cuts, 'of course there is no money left...' You can guess the rest.

Even *The Guardian* was starting to lose patience: 'The BBC is helping convince viewers that spending cuts are inevitable. It's a large-scale version of peer pressure.'[149] If you say something often enough, people will believe it. We wrote to a senior BBC Executive to point this out and ask why an alternative view is not given an adequate airing. After all, Professor Christopher Pissarides, a UK economist from the London School of Economics, had told us that 'the Chancellor has exaggerated the sovereign risks that are threatening the country,'[150] and he was the 2010 Nobel Prize winner for economics. She begged to differ: 'I think, that there has to be some deficit reduction at some time. There is no Westminster political consensus on timing, but there is on the fact that spending cuts should provide the dominant form of deficit reduction.' We weren't asking for the BBC's economic position and anyway the BBC Charter states that 'our output is forbidden from expressing the opinion of the BBC on current affairs or matters of public policy'.[151] But the Executive goes on to tell us that 'my understanding is that the debt was only brought down to manageable levels through fiscal austerity in the 19th century and a combination of fiscal austerity and serious inflation in the 20th'. So we weren't really asking more than what the BBC expects of itself. But what this revealed was the core of the BBC analysis of the economic crisis, which also sets the parameters for what they consider to be this elusive mainstream 'academic strands of thinking'.

In the Executive's defence, it is hard for her to be impartial when there is only one view being put forward. But having said that, we refer to the BBC's own editorial guidelines: 'We will ask searching questions of those who hold public office and others who are accountable, and provide a comprehensive forum for public debate.' Perhaps she could forward that to Andrew Marr.

Christopher Pissarides was, and is still not, the only economist to raise doubts about the cuts narrative – his expertise, incidentally, is on 'job creation and job destruction'. In fact he wasn't even the only Nobel Prize-winning economist to question austerity. 'I think it is likely that the economic downturn will last far longer and human suffering will be all the greater,'[152] wrote Professor Joseph Stiglitz, who won his Nobel prize in 2001 and was Chief Economist at the World Bank. Or how about Professor Paul Krugman, from whom we heard earlier: 'Jobs now, deficits later was and is the right strategy. Unfortunately, it's a strategy that has been abandoned in the face of phantom risks and delusional hopes.'[153] He won the Nobel Prize in 2008. Is this part of 'every single strand of academic thinking' that the BBC News Executive was getting at? When we now know that the economic plans laid out in 2010 have stagnated the economy, created higher unemployment, reduced public services and increased borrowing, these views look increasingly mainstream.

And it wasn't Nobel Prize winners alone that were sceptical about this 'political consensus'. Remember our mention of Andrew Tyrie, the Conservative Chair of the Treasury Select Committee, who had upbraided George Osborne after his big budget speech in 2010. He accused Osborne that he had 'over-egged it', when he said that we were on the brink of bankruptcy? Even Martin Wolf, the Chief Economics Editor of the *Financial Times*, is a sceptic of the cuts narrative: 'It is a scandal that in an exceptionally severe downturn, the Treasury, in its majestic unwisdom, slashed its investment so deeply. Penny wise, pound-foolish does not come close to it.'[154] He goes on to ask, 'why is the government determined to stick to its plans even though the weak economy has led to far higher borrowing than originally expected?'[155] Neither he nor Andrew Tyrie can be accused of being part of the academic strand. Even the Conservative Party London Mayor Boris Johnson joined in, because he 'would like to see a very aggressive campaign for more investment in infrastructure,'[156] and we know there is only one place that this can come from – borrowing.

Nevertheless, we continued to voice our concerns on *Your Call* on Five Live, *You and Yours*, *Any Answers*, in letters to *The Guardian*, e-mails and complaints until we eventually received a seven-page letter from the Head of Editorial Standards at the BBC Trust, Francesca O'Brien. '…it is my view that the Today Programme and the BBC is not required to cover the countervailing view within or alongside items on the deficit and on the spending review and cuts in order to achieve due impartiality'. But how else can it be done?

This helps to explain how the BBC has become a debt storyteller and protector of the single narrative. And it is not just the BBC. The same sins of journalistic bias underpin reporting on Sky, ITV and other TV news channels, almost all UK newspapers and radio news platforms.

With few exceptions, journalists and the media are the voice of the single debt narrative, carrying it into our homes and into our heads. We saw in the last chapter that what a senior BBC Executive calls 'extremes of academic opinion' are in fact the economics of social justice that were started with Adam Smith, worked their way to John Maynard Keynes and are reflected in the views of Nobel Prize-winning economists today. These economists may be 'outliers' in what the BBC thinks of as mainstream economic thinking – but they are in no sense 'outliers' in the world of economics. They are its leaders.

Stephanie Flanders is the Economics Editor of the BBC, yet, as we saw, she worked for four years as a speechwriter for Larry Summers. Larry was the Treasury Secretary in the United States government who oversaw and pushed for the Gramm-Leach-Bliley Act, which allowed banks to combine retail and investment activities under one roof. As we read in an earlier chapter it was only after this act was passed that the likes of RBS were allowed to owe thirty-five times more money than that which they had in reserve. This was a key piece of legislation that created the conditions for the credit crunch. Does that not give her a specific insight into the aftermath of this deregulation and the subsequent period of austerity? Did that not teach her to be sceptical? Is that why she decided to use two minutes and thirty seconds of her September 2011 report on poor economic growth to speak about the impact of the Japanese tsunami, a bank holiday for the royal wedding and bad weather?

You could accuse Evan Davis of not being neutral either. He worked for the Institute of Fiscal Studies and wrote a book promoting the privatisation of the public sector. He is now reporting on significant cuts to the public sector. Does that colour his analysis? Perhaps not. But is he selective about his line of questioning because, as he admitted to us, the 'existence of a deficit problem' is 'obscure' and covering it 'might confuse things'? Subjecting the rationale for dismantling the welfare state and swathes of the public sector to public debate might 'confuse things'?

We are not suggesting that the likes of Stephanie Flanders or Evan Davis are biased. They are seasoned, respected journalists, but they are knowledgeable enough to know better, and knowledgeable enough to ask politicians better questions – as their own editorial standards demand. They should, or rather must, be aware of the information presented in this book, sufficient to inform their critical enquiry of government and opposition political spokesmen and women. After all, they have the access and the opportunity to ask politicians questions on our behalf. The more interviews pass without challenging questions, the deeper we sink into democratic crisis.

But this is where the single narrative is, and journalistic questioning seems to have hardly got beneath the surface of the key tenets of the narrative economyths – 'we are on the brink of bankruptcy', '£120m per day to pay off our deficit', 'our triple A credit rating is under threat', 'we could end up like Greece', and so on. There seems to have been a collective suspension of disbelief amongst journalists at every level of editorial seniority and in every form of the media. The likes of Polly Toynbee, Will Hutton, Aditya Chakraborrty and Martin Wolf stand out from the media crowd, but they are lone voices.

We hope this book has taken you on a journey through the single debt narrative that has a stranglehold on the debate and discussion about the economic situation we are in. We are not saying there has not been an economic crisis in the country or that there is no debt and no deficit. What we're trying to show is that there is an alternative way of looking at it that does not involve wholesale, structural and fundamental change to our society and the things in it we value – enough of a counter-argument to stage a public debate about these historic events that are changing the very fabric of Britain. Our argument is that these changes are not being made for economic reasons, but for political and ideological reasons, or as Thatcher put it 'for the heart and soul'. The problem is the technical nature of the economics debate and the overwhelming influence of one philosophy of economics is preventing us from asking these fundamental and important questions. This is happening in our name. What we need to be asking and what we need to be making our journalists ask, is what is all this austerity for? What will our country look like at the end of it? These are the questions of the day. Moral, not economic questions – and so, open to argument.

You may disagree with our debt and deficit analysis, but the impacts of the cuts are undeniable. The latest addition to the tainted, self-indulgent world of banking are food banks. We now have emergency food-handouts in the world's seventh largest and richest economy – more than 200 of them across the UK. The Trussell Trust estimates that in 2011–2 food banks fed 128,687 people nationwide, 100 per cent more than in the previous year. Food banks are opening at a rate of three per week.

Caroline Spelman, Secretary of State for Environment, Food and Rural Affairs, thinks that 'no one will argue with the role of food banks, which are an excellent example of the big society'.[157] Do you think that food banks are an 'excellent example' of *anything*? Around 43 per cent of visitors to Trussell Trust distribution centres nationwide come because of changes to their benefits or a crisis loan being refused.[158] There are caps on benefits, withdrawal of benefits for people with disabilities, and in 2013 there will be a 'bedroom tax' that will threaten the 660,000 social tenants with the loss of their houses. Also in 2013 people on benefits may well have to contribute to council tax, which will make a straight choice between heat, eat and tax. What would you do? This is in the name of deficit reduction. Is this the society we want?

We have seen that our national debt is not historically high at all. George Osborne reluctantly confirmed that. Our deficit is high, yes, but it was caused by a gap in income tax receipts due to the finance sector-inspired recession and twenty-five years of shifting from a 'high-tax/high-wage' economy to a 'low-tax/low-wage' economy. It was not caused by 'overspending' on public services, and even Mervyn King, the country's chief banker, confirmed that. But there is a strong argument that the deficit is manageable and can be addressed through a complex of options that could include growth, taxing the better off, taxing financial transactions and borrowing for investment – and allowing inflation – amongst other things. We have also learnt that there are two broad strands of economics, one based on social justice that was dominant up until the 1970s, and the other based on merit and accumulating personal wealth. The latter is the dominant force in economics today.

In the previous chapter we have seen that the shift in economic policy from pre- to post-1970s was precipitated by a change in political thinking. The scale of change our country is undergoing is fundamental, and some of it, like the change in the National Health Service, has a tenuous link to public funding. These are not decisions made by economists. These are decisions made by politicians, and for at least some MPs from the Conservative and Liberal Democratic parties, as Alan Johnson observed, 'this [cutting public spending] is what they came into politics for'.

So, we are making the case that cuts and austerity ride on the back of a 'single narrative', the only story in town – that we are supposedly in economic 'crisis'. That's a very successful narrative, indeed. It drives almost everything. But narratives have to be created, and we have seen that it is the politicians and economists who do the creating. But then they have to be sold, and we have seen that this has been the job of the media – most prominently the BBC – which has done the hard work of 'making the pitch' and driving the message home, day after day.

If nothing else, we hope that this book offers a reasoned argument that there is an alternative narrative. We have witnessed how it does not get the airing with the same authority or presence as the debt crisis story and the cuts story. Not that this has not happened before. Tony Blair's government pushed the single narrative of weapons of mass destruction in Iraq. We were asked to believe this to be true even in the face of the person who was in Iraq looking for the weapons, Hans Blix, who told us they didn't exist. Political narratives are powerful aren't they? They can overwhelm contrary evidence. On that occasion John Humphrys stoutly and relentlessly challenged the narrative – which eventually fell apart. How are editorial decisions made about which narratives to challenge and which to leave run?

So why do we fall for these narratives? After all, an economic story may be sold, but it has also to be *bought,* and that is not necessarily a passive thing, either. It has been bought by the electorate, by us. Survey after survey has shown that there is majority support for the cuts programme. It may be diminishing as they bite, but the support is enough to push the programme through. How come?

We can be deceived into believing things, people can be frightened into going along with schemes that are not even in their best interest. Scare stories about debt and deficit under-mining our way of life, launching us into that terrifying state, even bankruptcy, were enough to scare anyone into believing that cuts were 'necessary' and 'unavoidable'.

Others say it is out of fear of the high levels of uncertainty that abound these days. Our lives are so full of risk and unpre-dictability that we huddle around authoritarian figures for a sense of security. Is this why we admire people like Richard Branson, one of those British 'oligarchs' who are buying up state assets and the public sector? Or maybe we are suffering from a collective sense of guilt at having enjoyed the excesses (some of us, at least) of the last ten or fifteen years, and so we are willing to 'take the medicine'. Remember, Cameron, amongst others, tries to make us feel guilty for leaving our children with the national debt.

A darker thought is that we try to shift that sense of guilt by blaming it on the poor. That the awful reality of growing poverty stares us in the face on the streets and from the TV, and we cope with it by going along with the idea that the poor are scroungers, that they bring it on themselves, that they are frauds. But some people are simply persuaded that austerity is actually a good thing and that pain now is necessary for good times later. Rather them than us.

So who is reading this book? A banker – shamed or still conceited? A single mother or a disabled person struggling with collapsing benefits? An economist stunned or excited by the Mary Poppins world they helped to create? A public sector worker fearfully scanning the headlines to work out if they are likely to hold on to their job? A member of parliament trapped in the single narrative of deficit-reduction? Whoever you are, you may be reading this as an observer. But you can't just be an observer of the cuts programme. There is such a thing as society and there really is a sense in which 'we are all in this together' – however fragile our democracy, the government still belongs to the citizen and their acts are still carried out with our consent. So where is the reader in all of this?

No one is saying that reducing, even dismantling and privatising the public sector is not a legitimate point of view, but as we have said before, so is the alternative that argues this is wrong, even counter-productive. It is just that the bankruptcy, credit rating, debt and deficit mantras stop us from debating whether this is what we want for our country or not. So whether you consider there is a debt/deficit crisis or not will largely come down to your political point of view. We are entitled to think that there is no need for large scale cuts without being considered a heretic, a lunatic or, as Martha Kearney of Radio Four would say, a deficit 'denier'. Otherwise we enter more deeply into democratic crisis.

What we want to know is what is our society going to look like once this crisis is over? It is exactly the same question that our predecessors asked in 1945 – and answered it with the world's most advanced social safety net, universal, free health-care and education, a new motorway and rail system, an expansionary university sector. And let us be clear that the austerity that the country is experiencing now is making cuts to our National Health Service, schools, benefits system and pensions that may not easily be undone, once the deficit receded. What is happening now will be a platform for the next ten or twenty years, and when we emerge from this period we risk seeing a smaller public sector, shrunken local councils, a withered local democracy, only basic social and care services, a less-than-subsistence benefits system, increased poverty and a bigger gap between the rich and the poor. If that is the vision we are being sold through the debt narrative – let's debate *that*.

Acknowledgements

In the seminal 1980s TV series *Boys From the Black Stuff*, which dramatised the bitter struggle of working people against the tide of Thatcherism, Christy's wife berates him for not fighting: 'Why don't you fight back – they're knocking the shite and the stuffing out of you!'[159] The scene was emblematic of how unequal struggles by men and women alike are embedded in family solidarity. The back-story of this book and the campaign it celebrates is one of just such family solidarity. Barry and Saville were urged on and supported by Joann and Ame, two great fighters, optimists themselves and inspiring partners.

A number of other fighters have been inspirational, not least Polly Toynbee who, almost alone, has had the moral courage and insight to document from its inception the unfolding social tragedy that is Britain's austerity programme. There are those who retain their integrity in these distorting times and who also, sometimes unknowingly, were intellectual mentors: Michael Blastland and Will Hutton, and also Perry Walker at the New Economics Foundation who provided critical but supportive feedback on the underlying economic analysis of alleged 'crisis'. Professor Oliver Penrose joined our analysing for a brief period and provided a critical check on some runaway ideas.

Other fighters who gave energy to the campaign that culminates in this book are our parents, Minnie and Ike Kushner whose principled social justice was expressed in a family upbringing that was laced with an insistence on fairness and honesty; and Joe and Cath, Barry's parents-in-law, who spent their life fighting injustice, and our cousin Gerald with a wisdom from his lifetime's work in teaching social justice as a Jewish, Buddhist, Marxist, humanist.

Our families' drive for social justice is now joined by the next generation – by Louis, Isis and Katie, and Elliot and Olie. They must strive to do a better job than our generation.

This book is the culmination of a two-year campaign, a celebration of brotherly accomplishment and a seamless comingling of ideas. Nonetheless, its unique narrative style, its data reach and its vision is down to Barry who, as lead writer and editor, brought an unrelenting commitment and energy to its completion.

Notes

1. *http://www.hm-treasury.gov.uk/press_05_10.htm*
2. *ibid.*
3. *The Andrew Marr Show,* 20 June 2010
4. *The Guardian,* 4 November 2010
5. http://news.bbc.co.uk/1/hi/8587877.stm
6. http://news.bbc.co.uk/1/hi/8587877.stm
7. Mervyn King giving evidence to the Treasury Select Committee, 1 March 2011
8. http://www.telegraph.co.uk/news/politics/5674916/Ed-Balls-no-cut-in-spending-despite-soaring-debt.html
9. *The Guardian,* 20 June 2010
10. http://www.bbc.co.uk/news/10088172
11. Treasury Select Committee, 4 November 2010
12. Email from Senior BBC Executive to Saville Kushner, 9 September 2011
13. *ibid.*
14. Email from Evan Davis to Barry Kushner, 12 January 2011
15. *The Guardian,* 8 February 2011
16. *Financial Times,* 18 February 2010
17. *The Guardian,* 3 March 2010
18. Daily Mirror 9 January 2011
19. Treasury Select Committee, 4 November 2010
20. http://www.youtube.com/watch?v=Y8JcZl5CcD0; http://bristol.indymedia.org/article/703498
21. *The New York Times,* 24 March 2011
22. www.hm-treasury.gov.uk/spendingreview_introduction.html
23. www.bbc.co.uk/news/business-13200758
24. http://economics.about.com/cs/economicsglossary/g/gdp.htm
25. http://financial-dictionary.thefreedictionary.com/GDP
26. *The Andrew Marr Show,* 7 October 2010
27. David Cameron's speech to the Conservative Party conference, 7 October 2009
28. news.bbc.co.uk/1/hi/business/8403286.stm
29. www.debtbombshell.com/
30. http://www.econlib.org/library/Topics/HighSchool/BudgetDeficitsandPublicDebt.html
31. Public sector finances: Public sector finances excluding financial interventions, Office of National Statistics
32. www.guardian.co.uk/uk/2004/mar/05/health.drugsandalcohol
33. www.ercouncil.org/chart_of_the_week.php?subaction=showfull&id=1331902003&archive=&start_from=&ucat=3&
34. 'Government and public sector debt measures', Office for National Statistics
35. http://www.guardian.co.uk/business/2010/mar/03/history-lessons-on-public-debt
36. David Hume 'Of Public Credit', 1742
37. www.ukpublicspending.co.uk
38. David Hume 'Of Public Credit', 1742
39. ibid.
40. http://www.bbc.co.uk/news/uk-politics-17661004
41. Email to Evan Davis, 21 January 2011
42. Email from Evan Davis, 21 January 2011
43. Alistair Darling, *Back from the Brink,* 2010
44. *Today* programme, 27 May 2010

45. Vince Cable interviewed on *Newsnight*, 25 May 2010
46. George Osborne, Mais Lecture, 24 February 2010
47. *The Guardian*, 20 May 2011
48. *Financial Times Lexicon*
49. Alistair Darling, *Back from the Brink*, 2010
50. ibid.
51. *Investors Chronicle*, February 2010
52. 'Britain's "structural deficits" disease', *The Financial Times*, 4 March 2010
53. Alistair Darling, *Back from the Brink*, 2010
54. http://en.wikipedia.org/wiki/Keynesian_economics
55. http://www.english.rfi.fr/economy/20100331-frances-budget-deficit-hits-record-high
56. IFS Survey of the UK Tax System, November 2011
57. http://conservativehome.blogs.com/leftwatch/2011/06/labour-peer-blames-overspending-under-labour-for-the-recession.html
58. liberalconspiracy.org/2011/06/12/vince-cable-opens-up-a-big-dividing-line-with-osborne-on-the-economy/
59. George Osborne, Budget Speech 22 June 2010
60. George Osborne Spending Review Statement, 20 October 2010
61. Alistair Darling, *Back from the Brink*, 2010
62. http://www.scotland.gov.uk/Publications/2011/06/21144516/7
63. Mervyn King's Address to the TUC conference, 15 September 2010
64. Mervyn King giving evidence to the Treasury Select Committee, 2 March 2011
65. Coalition Agreement, 12 May 2010
66. David Cameron, CBI Annual Conference, 29 November 2009
67. D. Webb & J. Bardens, 'Government borrowing, debt and debt interest payments: historical statistics and forecasts', House of Commons Library, May 2012
68. www.ft.com/cms/s/0/09b66e60-dd4e-11df-9236-00144feabdco.html#axzz1YmRIg7sx
69. http://www.guardian.co.uk/news/datablog/2011/jan/13/interest-rates-uk-since-1694
70. *The New York Times*, 24 March 2011
71. *Financial Times Lexicon*
72. Adam Smith, *Wealth of Nations*, 1776
73. http://www.cablegatesearch.net/cable.php?id=10LONDON364&q=king%20mervyn
74. http://www.guardian.co.uk/commentisfree/2010/dec/01/mervyn-king-bank-of-england
75. http://www.guardian.co.uk/commentisfree/2010/jun/22/budget-taxandspending
76. *Human Development Report*, United Nations, December 2010
77. *An Overview of Child Well-Being in Rich Countries*, Report Card #7, Innocenti Research Centre, UNICEF, 2007
78. www.independent.co.uk/news/uk/politics/mps-hit-out-at-vodafone-tax-letoff-6258782.html
79. www.independent.co.uk/news/uk/politics/mps-hit-out-at-vodafone-tax-letoff-tax 6258782.html
80. www.telegraph.co.uk/finance/newsbysector/banksandfinance/8348764/Lloyds-will-not-pay-corporation-tax-until-profits-hit-15bn.html
81. www.bbc.co.uk/news/business-17187277
82. www.guardian.co.uk/world/2010/nov/29/philip-green-protest-alleged-tax-avoidance
83. *The Missing Billions: The UK Tax Gap*, TUC, 2011
84. *The Size of the UK Outsourcing Market – Across The Private And*